Absent

How to Heal from Emotionally Toxic Parents - A Grown-Up's Guide to Healing from Childhood Neglect, Manipulation, Trauma, and Abusive Emotional Behavior

Olivia K. Rice

© Copyright 2020 - All rights reserved.

The content contained within this book may not be reproduced, duplicated or transmitted without direct written permission from the author or the publisher.

Under no circumstances will any blame or legal responsibility be held against the publisher, or author, for any damages, reparation, or monetary loss due to the information contained within this book, either directly or indirectly.

Legal Notice:

This book is copyright protected. It is only for personal use. You cannot amend, distribute, sell, use, quote, or paraphrase any part of the content within this book without the author or publisher's consent.

Disclaimer Notice:

Please note the information contained within this document is for educational and entertainment purposes only. All effort has been executed to present accurate, up-to-date, reliable, complete information. No warranties of any kind are declared or implied. Readers acknowledge that the author is not engaged in rendering legal, financial, medical or professional advice. The content within this book has been derived from various sources. Please consult a licensed professional before attempting any techniques outlined in this book.

By reading this document, the reader agrees that under no circumstances is the author responsible for any losses, direct or indirect, that are incurred as a result of the use of the information contained within this document, including, but not limited to, errors, omissions, or inaccuracies.

Table of Contents

Table of Contents 3
Introduction 7
Chapter 1: Say Whoa to The Quo! 14
    Status Quo: A Battle Between Inner Authenticity and World Messaging 14
    What's Going On? Deeper Insights on Childhood Trauma 17
    Why Do Our Traumatic Childhood Experiences Linger So Long? 20
    Illusive Forms of Emotionally Toxic Parenting 29
    Effects of Abuse on Your Adult Life: 36
    Sweetheart, It Was Not Your Fault 39
    One step Closer To Acceptance 40
        Three main keys to cultivate acceptance: 45
        Some tactics to work towards accepting a difficult situation: 47
    My Healing Contract 54
Chapter 2: My toxic parent 55
    So, What Is A Toxic Parent? 55
        Godlike Parents 56
        The Inadequate Parents 58
        The Controllers 60
        The Verbal Abusers 61

The Physical Abusers 64
The Alcoholics 65
The Sexual Abusers 66
Why Do Parents Behave This Way? 67
Types of Child Abuse 73
    Physical 75
    Mental 76
    Verbal 78
    Emotional 80
    Financial 83
    Sexual 85
    Spiritual 87
Is Abuse Biologically Hereditary? 89
So what now? 92
    Main ways how toxicity is handed down: 93
Things to Recognize on The Path to Healing 96
Strategies to Get Unstuck 103
Reflection 106

Chapter 3: A Safe Space For Healing 109
Safe Space 110
    What is it? 110
    Why do I need it? 110
    How do I create it? 111
Empathy vs. Sympathy 117
    4 Steps to Self-Empathy 118
Importance of Self-Regulation 120

Additional Tips for Recovering From Trauma: 122
Chapter 4: To cut or not to cut the ties? 125
    It's okay to cut the ties with your parents: 126
    It's also okay if you don't cut the ties: 130
    Setting healthy boundaries 133
        How to Set Healthy Boundaries 133
        Benefits of Healthy Boundaries 134
        Tips on Building and Preserving Your Boundaries . 135
        Boundaries and Consequences 136
    Common Tactics of Manipulative Parents 137
    Writing Exercise: Pros and Cons of Cutting Ties 138
        Should I Cut Ties With My Parents? 139
Chapter 5: Oh, my feelings! 140
    Self-Blame 143
        How to deal with self-blame: 145
        Shame vs. Guilt 146
    Anger 147
        How can post-traumatic anger become a problem: 148
        How to express anger in a healthy way: 150
        Anger Management: Practical Tips: 152
    Sadness And Grief 152
        Grief And Its Stages 153
        Important Things To Grieve 155
Chapter 6: A self-loving you 157
    Dissecting Limiting Beliefs 158
    Hey, Little One: Reconnecting With Your Inner Child 159

Who Is My Inner Child?...159
Steps To Connect With Your Inner Child: 160
How do I Know if my Inner Child is Wounded?....... 161
Indulging in Self-Love 162
The Four components of Self-love:.........................163
A Prescription For Self-Love...................................164
Chapter 7: What About Forgiveness? 166
What Forgiveness Is..167
What Forgiveness Is NOT...167
Is Forgiveness Really Necessary? 168
Chapter 8: From Weakness to Strength - Finding Your Authentic Self..170
Contract: A New Relationship With You (The Real You) 172
Conclusion 174
References..175

Introduction

"The greatest burden a child must bear is the unlived life of its parents."

- Carl Gustav Jung

What do you recall when you think back to your childhood? Is it - family picnics, trips to the beach, and school concerts with your parents cheering loudly from the crowd? Or is it - family members yelling at each other, living in transition between your divorced parent's homes, and feeling like you never fit in or belong?

Now think about your adulthood up to this point. Do you feel overwhelmed with responsibility? Do you desire a connection but find it difficult to trust other people? Do you seek joy and peace but find yourself sometimes having emotional outbursts that seem to come out of nowhere?

Absent is about taking a look at your childhood from a non-judgmental perspective and exploring how those past events have impacted your adulthood. We all have an unconscious part of our minds that carry our unmet childhood needs and emotions. This part of our minds is called our inner child. Our inner child still operates within us and affects how we see the world - whether we realize it or not. I wrote this book to help you reconnect with your inner child's core needs to be seen, heard, and authentically expressed. When we are children, we don't have the emotional maturity to process and express our personal experiences. We rely on our parents to guide us through our emotions. However, our parents are flawed human beings - some more than others. Often, they are not emotionally mature or conscious enough to realize the extent of their absence in their child's emotional development. Absent will introduce you to the consequences of your parents not meeting your emotional needs as a child. I will show you how to identify the toxic impact that your parents may have inflicted upon you and will guide your inner child along a path of greater emotional maturity and healing.

As a start, I'm going to share a piece of my story with you. When I turned six, mom started up her own real-estate business. She said she grew up with nothing and would gain everything she wanted in this new role. Her career became an obsession and money, her biggest motivator. "Olivia, I want the best. And I want you to have it too." But what did "the best" mean to Mom? A new SUV, designer clothes, and of course; the perfect husband and daughter.

Dad just couldn't live up to her strict standards and left. I remember her words when she found out he was remarrying. "He's weak, Olivia. Don't you ever settle for less than perfect. He decided to settle for a plain housewife who will die washing his laundry. One day he will realize what he left behind. I know that you will never leave me behind because you know who provided for you, who really loves you, and who is paying for your education."

I also remember her getting up at 4.30 a.m. for an exercise session with her personal trainer, but never arising early for a cuddle session with me... "No time for such neediness. Grow up, Olivia."

Even though she was sitting at a desk, she always seemed elegant, tall and strong to me. I wanted to be and look just like her. I would try and draw or make notes (though I couldn't even write yet), just like she did. I would mimic her movements and the way she talked on the phone. "Are you mocking me, Olivia? Stop it. You're distracting me and wasting my paper. My dreams have been on hold since you were born, and now I'm getting them back and building an empire for you. Don't cry. I'm teaching you to follow your dreams no matter what. Pull yourself together."

So I pulled myself together – every single day. Not only did I grow up, but I also grew to perfect, perform and persist. I pushed through until I became - by all appearances - an incredibly successful businesswoman. I worked 14-hour days for 15 years to become one of the highest-paid and most reputable female consultants in my field. I maintained a strict diet and exercised through it all. "The world doesn't like fat women, Olivia. Men have no desire for someone who is only pretty 'on the inside.' It's a lie. Your dad settled for that plump woman because she is just as weak and lazy as he is."

I was nominated for an award by a client after transforming their office culture into one of peak performance. The phone rang. It was Mom. "I hear you received an award."

"Well, I haven't received it, but I am one of a handful of women who have been nominated, Mom."

"In that case, it seems my congratulations has been premature. What's the point? Did my teachings on being the best go to waste?"

"Is that it, Mom? I'm hanging up now. I'll see you at Christmas." At that moment, it hit me. All this time, I have been "pulling myself together" and working towards "the best" when all I really wanted to win was Mom's approval. And this was my reward: a 30-second phone call and a half-hearted congratulations?!

I had to face the truth: Mom was a narcissist and had never cared about my well-being in the first place. And I have been carrying the burden of the unlived life inside of her since age six. I was in my early 30s now. Perfect on the outside, but inside, I was exhausted and lonely. I longed for a sense of family. I wanted intimacy, but I had no idea of what that even really meant. I had no real friends. I spent the majority of my 20s and 30s getting artificially high on a mix of sex, drugs, and alcohol, to numb the emptiness inside and mask the overwhelming pressure to perform. I was a mess, and I knew it. Something had to change.

They say you can choose your friends, but you can't choose your family. I get that. But seeing how I could change a company culture, I thought perhaps I could change my family by selecting a new way of thinking. Maybe I could choose a partner who would cultivate a different family environment from the one in which I grew up. But where does one even start? Well, the companies that wanted change called in an expert. So I accepted that I simply did not have the insight or strength to face the journey on my own. I was too exhausted from carrying a load that was not mine in the first place. Thinking back, I really did not even know where my dreams started and my Mom's drive and expectations for me ended.

For the first two years after that call, I worked closely with a psychologist specializing in childhood trauma and re-parenting techniques. The work we did together has transformed my life. Today, I'm 45, happily married and a mom with a purpose. My healing journey inspired me to continue studying trauma and for the past seven years, I've been coaching adults to release their suffering and live toxicity-free lives.

But why write a book about it? I've seen so many adults carry unfair burdens due to their parents' emotional absence and unlived lives. The most significant limitation of them all is our unresolved trauma, which can show up in so many ways. The impact of emotional abandonment and childhood trauma disguises itself. It can be hidden in our thinking patterns and behaviors.

This is why so many people walk this earth without figuring out why they are in pain.

In this book, I expose the toxicity that results from emotional abandonment and childhood trauma. I identify how the parent, who was supposed to be the adult that guides you to emotional maturity, may have failed. Then, I show you how to grow into an adult that shows up to meet the hidden needs of your abandoned inner child. My goal is to stop your silent suffering nestled in the belief that something is wrong with you. Together, we will shift your focus away from the limiting beliefs you have formed as a child. I will give you an exact blueprint you can use to understand better how your toxic parent neglected you. If you are not aware of how your parents were absent in your emotional development, you will never be able to truly heal.

It may sound confusing, but think about my life as an example: my mom provided me with "everything" you could ever ask for. She fed me healthy food. She paid for the best academic education. I never wanted for anything of monetary value. But my mom never saw my need for comfort and acceptance. I felt so guilty for wanting "more" when mom worked so hard to give me such a bountiful life. It led me to believe that I may never ask for any of my emotional needs to be fulfilled - by anyone. I always felt that I needed to achieve more so I can be worthy of affection. I grew into a highly functioning adult, that fell apart when I realized that all the monetary success or perfection in life would never fill my need for my mother's approval.

My work matters deeply to me because I am simply one of the millions of people who have been traumatized by something absent from their childhood. Every time we allow an adult to lighten their emotional load, we also ease the burden on the children who surround them. We break cycles. We change humanity for the better - one adult at a time. Our children, and this world, desperately need hope, light, and kindness. By the end of this book, you will have all the tools you need to self-heal your trauma and prevent your children from being negatively impacted by the unlived life inside of you! You will not be an adult who is emotionally unhealthy or absent.

Chapter 1:

Say Whoa to The Quo!

Status Quo: A Battle Between Inner Authenticity and World Messaging

No matter how different our stories might be I realized, through all my studies and counseling sessions, that there seems to be a status quo, an underlying dynamic in our stories. It seems that when our egos fail to achieve what they have been conditioned to believe as a need or a want, we see specific symptoms surface:

- Marital problems
- Physical symptoms like muscle stiffness or a frail immune system
- Unease or turbulence in our emotional lives
- Addictions
- Disruptive dreams

I've come to believe that these symptoms manifest as *issues* in our lives that cause some sort of suffering. However, we tend to miss that these symptoms serve to bring us to a halt. They ask that we start to pay attention. When was the last time you took a moment to ask what *issues* life is bringing to your attention so you can have a more in-depth look?

Being creatures of adaptation, humans tend to acclimatize to the messages that the world communicates to us. We then internalize the agendas in these messages. If we are lucky, the messages work in our favor and are aligned with our inner authenticity. Unfortunately, this is seldom the case because we are so overwhelmed by the world's messaging that we don't really know our authentic selves. If your authentic self is not aligned with the messaging you are internalizing, we start seeing the symptoms mentioned above.

When we become aware that we have an authentic truth within our being and start to engage the voice of our inner messaging with that of the world, we can begin to truly grow and evolve closer to our purpose on Earth. Only then can we enjoy a deeply, fulfilling journey in our life.

If we are not aware of or in touch with our inner authenticity, we can't distinguish between our true hearts' desires and the demands and agendas in the constant messaging we get from the world. If we can't identify the issues mentioned earlier as a symptom of inner-disconnect and frustration from our authentic selves, we will mistake these issues as our reality. As a result, we live our lives in a status quo of mediocrity, reacting to any emotional triggers and a general feeling of unease or unhappiness.

This might sound quite broad, and you may be wondering what the heck the world's messaging and your authentic truth has to do with healing wounds from your childhood or parents. Basically, when you're just a little kid, your parents are your world. They were the leading external messaging and reference points that you were exposed to when you started shaping your understanding and interpretation of how life and relationships function. The thing is, as we grow older, our relationship with our parents changes from child-to-parent into adult-to-adult. And this is where so much of our messaging and identity gets blurred.

The mere fact that you picked up this book shows that you are in a position where you can't yet fully pinpoint the extent to which your parents have influenced the symptoms or issues in your life. You are most likely aware of a problem in your relationship with them, and that may be causing troubles in your emotional lives, your own family, your own addictions, etc. But where does the burden and messaging of their unlived lives stop? Where does your authenticity start? Where did your parent(s) get stuck? When and where did they surrender their ambition for living a more fulfilling life?

In this chapter, I'll be guiding you into ways to see things from an objective viewpoint in order for you to make the connections you need to become more aware of what's really going behind the symptoms you are experiencing. After working through this chapter, you will have a deeper understanding of your internal conversation and will be able to guide your thoughts away from self-blame. This chapter will set you on the right path towards accepting your current situation as a means to deal with it properly. This chapter is all about your "Me-Talk." If you do not know who you are, you will adapt to any messaging coming your way.

So first off, we'll have a look at why childhood abuse and trauma is especially harmful in the way we learn to interpret the world. Then we take a peek into why our childhood wounds linger with us for most of our lives. After that, we look at different forms of toxic parenting, the effects thereof. That will aim to guide you into accepting that much of your childhood trauma, which manifests in various negative symptoms in your life, really wasn't your fault.

Ready? Let's dive in!

What's Going On? Deeper Insights on Childhood Trauma

Trauma and abuse in early childhood can cause immense harm. In the early years of childhood, our brains and our personalities are still in a developmental phase. Children are very dependent on their caregivers since they don't know how to take care of themselves. In addition to this, you'll find that children are like little sponges that absorb everything around them. However, they don't necessarily have the mental and emotional capacities to identify and distance themselves from what causes them harm. In terms of emotional harm, they also don't know what emotionally healthy behavior is and what isn't.

According to statistics published by DoSomething (one of the largest not-for-profit organizations exclusively for young people and social change, operating in the U.S. and in 131 countries around the world):

- 1 in 7 children in the US experienced child abuse or neglect in 2015.
- The most common form of child abuse seems to be neglect, followed by physical abuse, after that, sexual abuse and psychological abuse.
- In 2018, it was estimated that around 16 percent of abused children experienced maltreatment more than once and in different forms.
- Both boys (48.6 percent) and girls (51 percent) experienced childhood abuse at approximately the same rate. Therefore, childhood abuse doesn't show much gender preference.
- Children who come from families with a low socio-economic status showed child-abuse rates five times higher than those of families with a higher socioeconomic status.
- Children under the age of one were most vulnerable to neglect and mistreatment, accounting for almost half of child fatalities in the US from abuse in 2018.
- 76 percent of children who were victims of child abuse in 2018 were abused by their parents.

- Another shocking statistic in 2018 shows that 76 percent of children removed from their homes and placed in foster care were removed due to abusive neglect. That totals more than 160,000 children in that single year!
- Mental-health difficulties like depression, anxiety, bipolar disorder, PTSD, eating disorders, and substance abuse are more likely to manifest in the lives of adult survivors of childhood abuse.
- Adults who survived abuse as children are prone to engaging in high-risk activities and behaviors like drug use, reckless sex, and alcohol abuse. In addition to this, they are also reported to have lower general health levels than adults with no experience of childhood abuse.

If you've ever felt alone or isolated in your struggles, you are not alone. Secondly, I also urge you to realize how vital your healing is. Every person who recovers from childhood neglect and abuse can become a beacon of hope in the world. As in my case, my recovery empowered me to help so many other adults to heal and raise more conscious and enlightened generations after them. When we heal, a part of the world heals too.

Why Do Our Traumatic Childhood Experiences Linger So Long?

As children, we don't know any better than what we experience, especially in the case of a chronically abusive parent. If all we know or experience is the environment created by an abusive parent, children won't even question it. Only in time, and as they grow or even discover something different from that environment that has been their reality for so long, they may realize that there is an alternative reality to what they have lived so far. They may realize that what they know may not actually be healthy at all.

When children are still young, they assume their parents exhibit "normal" because that is the only reality they know - whether their parents are toxic or not. That behavior and environment is the status quo and seen as entirely normal. Without any existing basis for comparison, kids think other families operate by the same dysfunctional patterns as what happens in their homes. I was six and thought my mom's weekly planning session at the dinner table was just as fun and intimate as "Sunday lunch." I'm not saying that planning your week is not a good goal or that my mom's commitment was not admirable. At the same time, as a little girl, I had a much deeper need than just learning how to plan. I needed to learn how to process my emotions. I needed to learn how to connect to people. I needed to be held.

During a sleepover at a friend's home, her mom made us hot cocoa on Sunday morning. The house was filled with the smell of banana pancakes made by her dad. They listened to music and danced in the kitchen. I thought they were kind of nuts, but I felt so warm inside. I only asked Mom for pancakes on Sunday once and never again.

"Olivia, have you seen Lily's mom? Perhaps if she wasn't eating all those pancakes, she wouldn't have to push through the seating rows at the next school play like an ox," Mom chastised me at my request.

I grew to believe that to be true. Lilly's mom lacked discipline and was fat. Unlike my perfect mom and me, "her life was out of control." I started to believe that everyone's parents had to be cruel, unavailable, or controlling. Anything other than that demonstrated weakness and lack of self-control.

It is not possible to understand why bad things happen to us while we are still children. We don't yet have the means to seek professional help. The maturity or experience to differentiate between healthy and unhealthy behavior simply doesn't exist yet. Instead, children build coping mechanisms from an egoistic state to help them get by.

Unfortunately, in most cases, these coping mechanisms are rarely healthy and don't allow us to heal. Some of us even walk around as adults, still engaging in the coping mechanisms we instilled in childhood, without realizing that we use these systems to get us through life. If there is no form of intervention in an abused child's life, some form of corrective behavior or loving leadership and guidance, whatever behavior that child has instilled, is programmed into their behavioral patterns as "the norm."

In some cases, it's not even our childhood trauma that lingers, but rather the coping mechanism or the fundamental beliefs we locked down as children that shape our behavior. That is what stays. The glue that made the coping mechanism stick was the layers and layers of traumatic and abusive experiences that kept imprinting the relevance of these beliefs and behaviors to the point where it feels like it is a part of us.

One Friday, after a busy week, I felt the family (and myself) could do with a little takeout. As I walked into the pizza place, I couldn't believe my eyes. There she was, standing right in front of me: Karen, the girl who bullied me and made me cry nearly every day at middle school. Now almost 30 years later, she walked up to me with a smile on her face, telling me that she was a "big fan" of my counseling work and that she had attended a local seminar I had done a month earlier. I was shocked but not surprised because to treat me like she did when we were younger, she must have also been going through tough times at home. While we were waiting for our orders, I kept reminding myself that I was a professional and that Karen was no longer my childhood bully. I also realized that I wanted to know more about her. So I invited her to come home with me and join us for pizza night.

Karen told me that her husband of 12 years recently left her and attained custody of their two children. It seemed like she hadn't had a conversation in ages. The floodgates were open, and she just spilled out her heart to a girl she used to torment at school.

Karen ran her own highly successful PR firm and was earning top dollar. Her husband was a successful lawyer and wanted her to spend more time with their family and get a handle on her temper. He said he saw the damage that her absence, relentless criticism, and sudden outbursts were having on their children and their marriage. Karen was very aware that she had a bad temper since childhood, but she honestly felt that she was driving her family towards higher standards. It was not her intention to be critical. She just wanted to raise tough kids because the world can be so cruel.

As the night progressed, pizza night became an impromptu counseling session. I asked Karen to explain her thoughts on family life and how her parents were. She painted a perfect picture, especially when it came to her mother, an extremely successful lawyer. In fact, Karen proudly proclaimed that if it weren't for her mom, she would never have started her own PR firm. I asked her if her mother was still alive and what their relationship was like.

"Well, our relationship is pretty great. I mean, she pushes me and supports me to be a strong woman. You know, she became a lawyer and started her own practice at a time when gender equality was a completely foreign term. A woman's place was still

'barefoot and pregnant in the kitchen.' She had to work so hard to be respected and build a client base. No wonder she flipped when I mentioned that I want to sell my firm to spend more time at home and slow things down a bit. She said I'd be failing every other successful woman who has fought so hard to gain independence and run their own business. She mentioned that I'd be smashing every dream and aspiration she had for me and that no daughter of hers would make such a stupid decision to give up their career and become a housewife. What she said hurt, but then again, what do I know about running a household anyway? I mean, I'd probably waste my time and maybe my kids and husband would get irritated with my presence after a while. Perhaps they don't even want to spend more time with me... After all, my husband left anyway."

As Karen was telling me more about her mother, who was obviously not as superb as she was trying to make me believe, I picked up some behavior in her non-verbal communication: she had clenched her fists. When she caught herself doing so, she would open her hands and start rubbing her knees. I then asked if her mom had always been so oppressive and authoritarian.

"I wouldn't say so. I mean, I would get the odd spanking when I was out of line, like any other kid. But I wouldn't go as far as to say she was an oppressor or authoritarian. She was just making sure I grew into a woman with a backbone and not a wishbone."

When Karen started talking about spankings and her developing backbone, there was a slight change in her voice's emotional level. Eventually, she explained that "the odd spanking" was, in fact, a few harsh smacks with whatever was in her mother's sight - a wooden spoon, a ruler, or just a bare hand - up to three times a week. It didn't take much for Karen to get a solid physical or verbal slap. She could have made a mistake while helping out with a chore around the house, brought home a report card that wasn't up to Mom's standards or overslept before school. It became evident that her mom also didn't stick to a smack on the bottom. Any spot would do for a beating, whether it was her arms, back, or legs.

"It's not like my mom really beat me up. There was never blood or anything like that. She was just keeping me in line and making sure I don't slack. And I think I turned out pretty successful, right?"

After this rationalization of her mother's behavior, I asked her if she ever feared her mother.

"Actually, I was scared to death of her when she got like that. But isn't that how you earn respect? I mean, she was fighting for her spot as a female lawyer in a man's world every day. If she didn't fight or take a stance, how would she ever be noticed? Aren't you supposed to be scared of your parents anyway?"

I then took a leap and asked her if she thought that her children should feel that way about her and her husband. Karen couldn't look me in the eye and got very uncomfortable. Like I mentioned, her husband was a lawyer. I asked her: "If a child walked into your husband's practice with bruises on his body from a spanking by a parent, would he not be obligated to report it to the authorities or a social worker?" This was the tipping point for Karen.

Her eyes shot up with tears, and all she could utter was: *"I think the chili on my pizza is really stirring things up. My stomach is upside down and my emotions are too."*

Feeling defenseless, Karen tried to cover her real emotions with a joke. That night, this poor woman had become aware of the real source of her temper and her criticism. It was a long-hidden volcano waiting to burst open. As a child, she carried so much unexpressed anger against her mother that the volcano of emotions inside her would sporadically erupt or blow off some steam when she experienced some pressure as an adult.

Who was the victim of these outbursts? Her husband or kids. Karen was not a cruel or evil woman, but rather a battered little girl with some harmful, conditioned behavior that she unknowingly put in place to protect herself from the harsh reality of her mother's behavior.

After that evening, Karen became a great friend and we supported her along her healing journey. With so many blurred boundaries, I did not want her to confuse our unexpected friendship with counseling or therapy, so we decided to find her a psychologist. However, she wasn't the only one who gained something through our encounter; I gained an extraordinary friendship. The two of us could relate to each other since childhood and engage in constructive conversations about how we dealt with the trauma inflicted by our parents.

Karen's story has a few lessons:

- *We can be blind and unaware of our childhood trauma deep into adulthood.*
  Karen had to hit rock bottom and lost her family before realizing that something was wrong and that she needed to make some changes.
- *Traumatized children often recreate a home environment like the one they were raised in to feel a false sense of security.*
  Though Karen's husband was not her mother, it was quite convenient to blame everything wrong on his profession. Every time she was triggered into some form of anger, she could turn to him to take out her suppressed anger towards her lawyer-mom. Karen unconsciously created a familiar sense of family - no matter how warped the idea was.
- *A seemingly successful and functioning adult's life can be influenced and even controlled by an emotionally destructive parent.*
  Though Karen was successful on the outside, her thoughts and actions were still very much ruled by her mother's voice.

- *Professional support is not enough - you need a place of grace.*
  My journey with Karen reminded me of something personally significant. People in Twelve Step programs learn to call up a sponsor or get to a group meeting when they need support. They are urged to run to a place of grace. In a sense, both Karen and I became a place of grace to each other. Sometimes, I did not need to be a coach with all the answers. When I had a bad day or caught myself engaging in malicious behavior as a mom, I could ring Karen up and simply be a mother who needed to get a response from another parent who can relate to my struggle and help me back on track.
- *It's not too late to start healing.*
  Karen was 40+ when she started treating her unattended wounds.
- *Healing is contagious.*
  Our healing ignites healing in our relationships too. When Karen became aware of how her wounds manifested, she was open to change. Once she started acting consistently towards positive change, her husband was able to trust her again. Their relationship could recover and, consequently, her relationship with her children got better too.

Millions of people walk this earth with no idea why they feel like things aren't working out for them. Since working through my own healing and studies on childhood trauma and the impact of toxic parents, I've seen hundreds of people who have suffered an impaired sense of self-worth.

Why? Because, like myself and Karen, they either had a parent who would smack them on a regular basis, burdened them with too much responsibility, completely overprotected them, abused them sexually or verbally, loaded them with guilt, made inappropriate hurtful jokes, or just never had anything uplifting to say to them. Sadly, many of these adults, were harmed in some way as children, and seldom see or realize the connection between their parents and their problems. For them, it's a real struggle to see their parents' significant impact on their lives. Perhaps you may be one such person or you have already recognized that something is wrong, but you just can't put your finger on it.

Next up, we're looking at some forms of emotionally toxic parenting that may be deceiving.

Illusive Forms of Emotionally Toxic Parenting

The actual term "toxic parent" maybe a little indistinct because it can be defined in so many different ways. For the purpose of this book, we'll consider a toxic parent as a person who is narcissistic or who has other personality disorders or mental illnesses. They may also be an addict, behave abusively or emotionally immature in this context. Basically, they are parents who carry a promise of love and care but who simultaneously mistreat their children.

As I mentioned earlier, young children often assume that their parents are typical, whether they are toxic or not. However, once children are exposed to other families who may not be operating with the same dysfunctional rules as the child is used to, they may become aware that something is "off." A child will eventually notice that emotionally healthy parents will illustrate sincere concern for their children's feelings. They will support them in pursuing their dreams and not project their own unlived desires onto their child. They will apologize when they screw up and be willing to discuss problems respectfully. When a child notices this behavior in other families, they realize that their parents are different. But because they are still children, they are not yet equipped to know what to do with the realization that their parents are different. Some children have the resilience to explore the differences or seek help through a teacher or other adults. But in most cases, they will simply stick to what their parents teach them because that is the reality that the child lives in.

Remember how I noticed that my friend Lily's parents were different to mine? I enjoyed their presence and longed for such connection and joy. But when I returned to the "reality" of my home and my mother, I stuck to the beliefs my mother was teaching me. At that stage I had no idea of how immense the psychological damage and pain could be in the long run. My mom also had no clue; she still doesn't. Karen also never realized the ways in which her mother's parenting was harmful to her. The point is that there are other forms of toxic parenting besides battering and verbal abuse that we often don't recognize.

Don't get me wrong, I understand that most parents really try their best to give their children a happy and healthy upbringing. All parents make mistakes that may lead to some therapy sessions in their children's future. Just because someone becomes a parent doesn't mean that they are all of a sudden immune to human error. It's just that some parents, unfortunately, tend to go past the point of a mistake here and there. They lean towards the toxic category. Whether a parent is deliberately engaging in toxic behavior or not, some actions are just so damaging to a child's emotional and mental well-being that if the child is hurt in that way, they can be affected by it well into their adult lives.

However, you look at things, the first step to healing or dealing with your problems is to become aware that you actually may have a toxic parent. You also need to be able to identify the specific ways in which your parents are dysfunctional or emotionally unstable.

If your parent(s) abused power in any of these ways, they might be toxic to an extent:

- *Your parents never affirmed or praised you and were overly critical.*
  For some people, showing tough love is how

they feel like they are making sure their children will be able to take care of themselves in the future. Are you an adult who falls apart if you sense some sort of failure or rejection? The chances are good that you had a parent who toxically denied ever providing you with enough security and affirmation as a child. This doesn't mean that tough love is ineffective, but it definitely does not work with all people and it can't be the only approach an adult takes while raising their child. It's also important to note that our parents will criticize us from time to time. If they do not show you that you are folding the laundry improperly, you will continue doing it wrong in the future. But things become toxic when a parent is supercritical regarding every little thing their child does. This often leads to the child developing a very harsh inner critic and that can be crippling as they become adults.

- *They show no level of respect or kindness towards you.*
  Your parents put their own needs before yours and do not consider your feelings or the people around them. They tend to be quite disrespectful.

- *Your parents remain in an emotionally reactive state.*
  If a parent is toxic, they are likely to struggle with controlling their emotions. They are often

described as overly dramatic and unpredictable. After my parents divorced, my mom would accuse my father of trying to manipulate me into wanting to stay with him. It really wasn't the case. I loved her, but I was scared of her at times. When I felt sad because I missed my father, I could never anticipate her reaction. Sometimes she would cry and ask if her company wasn't enough. Other times she would be furious and command me to stop crying and toughen up. I never knew which emotion would be triggered when I showed emotion.

- *They blame you for their problems and mistakes.*
  Toxic parents do not take responsibility for their own behavior and will seldom acknowledge their role in the dysfunctionality of your family. They will blame everything on you as a child. And this can often carry on well into adulthood if a grown child never uses their capacity to stand up for their inner self who has adapted to this kind of abuse and accepted it as the status quo.

- *They make you fear them, sometimes pity them, and make sure to let you know that nothing you do is enough. You never feel safe with them.*
  When parents are toxic, they can be extremely demanding and expect of their kids to do

everything according to their needs and standards. They make sure that their kids know that there is no regard for anyone's schedule and priorities but their own. If you do not live up to their expectations, you will probably have fear instilled in some way, depending on the technique your parent uses. If you do not drop everything to help them, they may yell at you as punishment.

- *They are manipulative and controlling.*
  Twisting the truth to put themselves in a better light, using guilt, denial and trivializing things to their advantage, comes effortlessly to them. Toxic parents also want the upper hand and may use guilt and money to exert their power and control. Everything always happens when and how they want to happen - always on their terms.

- *They do not allow you to express negative emotions.*
  Some parents deny their children's emotional needs. The result is a child entering adulthood unable to express how they feel or what they want. Sometimes parents are well-intentioned in helping their children always see the positive side of things. But if a child is denied the opportunity to express any negative feelings or thoughts, they suppress it and feel pressured to always appear upbeat and perfect. Suppressing years of negative feelings may also lead to

depression and cause them to become adults who can't handle negativity.

- *They ignore healthy boundaries.*
  It's normal - even responsible - for a parent to keep an eye on their children. In some cases, a little "Sherlock Mom" may be in order just to keep them safe. But some parents just have no regard for any form of boundaries. Toxic parents may be caught opening their children's door without a knock. All these little acts, add up and make it hard for children to create, organize, understand and maintain healthy boundaries later in life.

- *They hold their children responsible for their happiness.*
  Some parents go around saying that they gave up so much of their life to have the child, but that it is okay because their child is now the source of all their happiness. This is a huge burden to place on a child. In some cases, the parent may see this proclamation as a compliment that is intended to be sweet and reflect how amazing that child is. However, no child should be allowed to feel like they are responsible for their parent's happiness. If a child is forced into such a situation, they may have trouble realizing that we are all responsible for our own happiness as we get older.

Did you recognize any of these traits or behaviors? If so, you may wonder, "What now?" You have taken the first step: becoming aware that you have a problem with a toxic parent and have suffered abuse in some form.

Next, we look at the effects of this abuse, so you can identify if any of these effects may have manifested in your life. Take it easy and be patient with yourself. We're taking it one step at a time here.

Effects of Abuse on Your Adult Life:

Most toxic parents will say that they love their kids and actually mean it. However, when it comes to loving children, there is so much more on the table than just expressing a feeling through words. To really love children is a way of behaving (Forward & Buck, 1989). But if a child does not learn the appropriate "way of behaving" that illustrates love, many other relationships in the adult life of the child may be impacted, even the one you have with yourself. Unfortunately, this mostly happens in a negative way.

Look out for these common examples of how an abusive or toxic parent's behavior can later affect your life (Kos, 2017):

- You find yourself constantly entering relationships where you engage with a toxic attachment style: anxious ambivalent, anxious-avoidant or anxious-disorganized.

- You fundamentally believe that when people get close to you, they will abandon you or hurt you in some way.
- In general, you seem to think and expect the worst from people and life.
- You have little knowledge as to who you really are and what you feel.
- You seem afraid that you won't be liked, whether you know your truth or not. You feel like a real version of yourself just isn't enough and you are never comfortable in your own skin.
- You suffer from impostor syndrome where you often feel like a fraud, no matter what the situation.
- Your emotions are intense and unpredictable to the point where you most often get angry or sad for no apparent reason.
- You seem to have trouble "switching off" and struggle to relax or have a good time.
- You are a perfectionist and can't deal with flaws, especially your own.
- You do not want to behave like your parents, yet you every now and then you catch yourself acting like they do.

It's also important to know that many toxic parents tend to mistreat their children well into adulthood. Have you experienced any of the issues below as an adult?

- Your parents still treat you like a child, even though you are grown up.

- If you make any big life decisions, your parents demand that it be run through them for approval first. If not directly stated in this manner, it is definitely implied through unconscious pressure.
- You have an intense emotional reaction when it comes to spending time with them, you may leave feeling sad, guilty, angry, etc. Or you may be nervous or anxious at the thought of going to visit them.
- You are afraid to disagree with your parents.
- You are often confronted by money manipulations in their presence.
- You feel responsible for the way your parents feel.
- You never feel like the things you do are enough for your parents.
- If you reflect deeply inside you, there is a hope that your parents may change for the better in the future.

All of these effects of childhood abuse and neglect tend to lead to feelings of low self-esteem or self-worth. In turn, this can lead to damage in your intimate relationships, lack of self-confidence, outbursts of rage, anxiety, procrastination and self-sabotage (to only mention a few). Due to the fact that children have a very limited perception of the world, no matter how abusive they may be, parents will remain the main source of love and comfort. This means that an abused child will have a very distorted idea of the world and the way they see themselves.

All healthy relationships, be they between adults or adults and children, require vulnerability, trust and openness, things that get completely destroyed in toxic families (Forward & Buck, 1989). But there is hope in healing. You do not have to stay stuck in this cycle of abuse.

Sweetheart, It Was Not Your Fault

As you know by now, toxic parents are excellent when it comes to blaming others - especially children - for their emotions and behaviors. But even though your parents may blame you, the truth is actually that it is not based on something you did. They have problems of their own that are just manifesting in grotesque ways.

You must acknowledge and internalize that your parents have significant problems, and are unlikely to change, in many cases. I urge you not to see this as a negative but rather something that paves the way to acceptance. Always remember that you were only a kid, a little sponge to the world around you. What ever happened to you, you wouldn't know better. The adults around you should have been responsible for you.

Recognize that you don't have any control over your parents' actions; they don't behave toxically because you're doing something wrong. Toxic parents usually grew up with toxic parents. A toxic family is usually passed on or inherited between generations. The toxic system is thus not something that parents invent, but rather a result of the accumulated feelings, rules and interactions that have been handed down from ancestor to ancestor (Forward & Buck, 1989).

We'll get into the psyche of and the different kinds of toxic parents you get in Chapter 2. For the aim of this chapter, all you need to know is that you can stop the generational repetition of toxicity in your family system. Now is the time to stop blaming yourself for things you cannot change in the past and take responsibility for your healing. Be patient with yourself. Everyone has their own recovery time. It's up to you to find a pace that works for you.

One Step Closer To Acceptance

Awareness leads to acceptance and acceptance to healing. My question to you is whether you are aware and ready to accept that you have been a victim of some form of childhood trauma. Are you ready to take responsibility for your healing?

If you hesitate when it comes to the aforementioned questions, I urge you to put this book down and take some time to reflect on everything we have covered. If you are not at a place where some form of acknowledgement and acceptance is on the table for you, it may be unwise to proceed as healing comes *after* acceptance. But who knows? Maybe you will have to work through this book several times before you can really heal. It all may depend on the extent to which you experienced your childhood trauma.

As I'm writing this paragraph, I suddenly thought of the story of American poet, memoirist and actress Maya Angelou. She wrote several volumes of autobiographical works that explore various forms of oppression- from economic and racial to sexual and child abuse. In 1967, she published her first autobiographical work *I Know Why The Caged Bird Sings*. In this book, she tells the story of her childhood where she spent most of her time in the care of her paternal grandmother in rural Stamps, Arkansas. Before Angelou even turned eight, the little girl was raped by her mother's boyfriend, Mr. Freeman.

After she testified against Freeman at his trial, he was convicted and sentenced, but released from jail. A few days later Freeman was found dead (likely murdered by Angelou's uncles as her memoir implies). Following the traumatic sequence of events, Maya silenced her voice for years. She would occasionally speak to her brother, Bailey. In her book, Maya explains the rationale behind her silence as follows: *"My seven-and-a-half-year-old logic deduced that my voice had killed him, so I stopped speaking for almost six years."*

I have no idea of the extent to which you may have been hurt. If this little girl remained silent for nearly six years to eventually accept that the rape and death was not her fault, you might want to really have a gentle conversation with yourself regarding the pace you will accept the trauma you've been through. After Angelou healed, she used her experience to become one of the world's greatest poets and teachers, and enrich millions of lives around the world. Who knows what awaits you beyond your pain? Only you will know. Only you hold that key. Only you can know when you are ready for healing and acceptance. Let me be quite frank: It won't be easy. But it will be worth it!

Keep in mind as you embark on this journey that acceptance is an invaluable tool for restoring your peace of mind. Even still, it's very stressful to have toxic parents or be abused. You will need strategies to help you cope with your parents' dysfunction going forward. This is especially true if your parents are still alive and possibly continuing with their toxic behavior. You need to be vigilant and mindful of the things that may be a hurdle to your healing:

- When you start dealing with traumatic experiences, feelings of guilt and shame are like a rocking chair: it will keep you busy, it may even be something you coddle, but it will not move you forward. Make a point of getting to know the things you feel guilty about or shameful about. It is often said that the actual trauma didn't hurt you as much as the guilt and shame that accompanies it. *"A child's perception of events is as important as what actually occurred. While a child's life may not have actually been in danger, the child may have seen it as life-threatening,"* (Harvard Health Publishing, 2019). We'll get a little deeper into this later in the book, but for now, to be on the lookout for the things you may feel guilty or shameful about. Don't let it hold you back. Rather, see it as starting points in mapping out your own route to healing.

- In the 2019 Harvard Health Publishing article on how past trauma can haunt your future health, researchers state that a person's risk for mental and physical health problems rise as the number of traumatic events experienced increases. In other words, someone with five traumatic experiences will have a higher chance of developing health issues than someone who had only one negative adverse childhood experience. The tricky thing is when we experience trauma, we tend to want to avoid thoughts, people and places that remind us about it. In a sense, we try to deny the severity of the past trauma(s). But the longer we deny these effects, the more trauma can happen to us and, due to the frequency and past unresolved trauma, we run a higher risk of health problems. Doesn't that make sense? Hence, I'm urging you to start on this journey at a pace that suits you, but just get started. The longer you wait, the greater your risk of health problems which can be quite traumatic and even act as a trigger for emotional reactions from past unresolved trauma.

- Also be cognizant of the fact that you may be unaware of the role that childhood trauma is playing in your life. You may not really have a clue as to how your past is actually affecting you. Because trauma causes pain, we tend to put defense mechanisms in place to guard us against stress. One of the barriers we erect to guard us is denial of the effects of past trauma on current health. We tend to normalize our past problems, just like Karen rationalized / normalized the way in which his father beat him.

- Make sure that you have a support system in place so that you are not tempted to give into peer pressure through not wanting to look weak or feel vulnerable in front of others. Healing is ultimately a personal thing, but it does help to have a small trusted network - or even just one close confidant to support you. For some reason, we find it easier to ask for help when we heal after a physical scar. Say, for example, you had a shoulder operation. It might be a little awkward, but you will ask someone to help you dress the wound and yourself. You literally can't do it alone. But for some reason when it comes to our emotional scars, which we can't see, we hesitate to seek help from someone who can reach the spots that need healing and offer support where we are weak.

Three main keys to cultivate acceptance:

By now, it should be evident that healing our childhood wounds is no easy task, nor is it impossible. Once we understand how our childhood traumas and the form they surface in, we must work on accepting them for what they are and how they have impacted us. There are three keys to accepting your childhood trauma (Johnson,2019):

1. *Investigate your levels of self-knowledge.*
   Before we can accept anything about ourselves, we need to actually know our inner selves. You can start by feeling your emotions as they currently occur in the moment. Observe them and accept them. Don't try to change them immediately, just sit with them. Once you are present in the emotion, take a step back and see if you can trace things back to the origin of the emotion. Where did the emotion come from? What triggered it? Do this exercise in a quiet place where you can feel safe to relax and really allow yourself to be physically present in your body - even if the sensation of the emotion may be painful.
   Learning the skill of acceptance, specifically in relation to trauma, can be challenging turf. You can only win the battle if you are comfortable with your own knowledge of your capabilities

on rough terrain. Schedule a few moments for you and your trauma where you can sit with it and get to know the person you have become because of it. You can even consider giving each of your traumas a name. Then you can sit with each different trauma, if you have more than one.

2. *Look out for the truth.*
   We need to develop the ability to see things for what they really are, especially after we spend so much time and energy seeing things as we prefer to see them. Eventually we lose track of what we are seeing; we can't distinguish between reality and our constructed narrative of reality. We allow our imaginations to run wild when it comes to dealing with our childhood traumas. If you really want to accept the past and its impact on your future, you need to work on seeing things for what they essentially are. You can't work on illusions or the version of events you wished had happened.

3. *Differentiate between acceptance and preference.*
   Acceptance does not mean that you prefer something or support it. We tend to resist acceptance because we feel it's a means of "giving in." It is crucial that you establish a clear understanding with yourself, that you are not endorsing something through accepting it.

> You are not saying that you prefer the conditions your toxic parents created in your life. You are however saying that "this happened, it doesn't define me and I'm moving on."

To accept who you are and where you are in your life at the moment, you need honest clear perspective on the true nature of your trauma and to realize that acceptance is not giving in. You are simply creating space for things to be as they are without creating a narrative that implies that you have some right or responsibility to control or change how things may have worked out otherwise.

Some tactics to work towards accepting a difficult situation:

Look, this is no secret I'm going to share with you: Life is not fair. In fact, it is more often than not actually very unfair. But you have the ability to accept that fact and, if you embrace this ability, you will be able to better navigate through rough patches in life.

First up, remember the importance of acknowledging your situation. Very often people just stay in denial and avoid the problem. But the longer you deny, the longer it will take to address your issues. Even if a situation seems overwhelming and unchangeable, simply acknowledging it can move you towards acceptance so you can move on. So, now some important tactics in the form of questions. Answer these once you have truly acknowledged your situation.

Are you ready to develop a practical plan?

Pull up a blank page and have a little brainstorming session with yourself. Write down all possible ways you can deal with your issues. Once you get those creative juices flowing, you'll probably realize that you may have more options for handling the situation than you thought. Make sure to set some time aside to really think about and dissect the issue at hand. Though the problem may not be able to be fixed, you need to remind yourself that you can develop a game plan to cope with the situation. Simple actions like thinking about who you can call to support you and help you to stay on track when you feel like giving up, go a long way when it comes to coping with ongoing situations.

Do you have enough support from people around you?

Sometimes to ask for help is the most courageous thing you can do. Do not be scared to seek help in a variety of ways when you are learning to cope with a difficult situation in life. Do you feel overwhelmed at work or by your household chores? Share in honest vulnerability with your partner what you are going through and ask for some specific help around the house so they know how to support you. We can't expect the people around us to just know exactly what we need. They are not mind readers. You will empower the people who love and care for you to support you more effectively if you tell them in which ways they can help you. This way your deeds will be met much faster and you get closer to healing. I mean, haven't you ever had a Band-aid that you just couldn't properly stick because of an awkward position for you to reach alone? It helps if you can ask a friend or someone close to stick on the bandage where you struggle to reach. Why not try this approach when it comes to our emotional scabs?

Are you aware of the things you cannot change?

It is crucial that you identify the things that are in your control and those that aren't. Why? Because if you cannot change a situation, you will always be able to change your attitude towards it. For example, if you lost your job because your boss was unfair, it won't help you if you sit and mope over the fact that you were treated unfairly. Like we mentioned earlier, life is not fair. The chances of you changing anything about the nepotism your boss had shown are very slim. Instead, you can change your attitude and jump into action by getting your resume out as soon as possible.

If you struggle to deal with the fact that your mom is an alcoholic, you need to realize that you are not responsible to make her change her behavior. It is her responsibility and if you had numerous attempts to get her through rehab, it is okay to step back and let her deal with the repercussions of her behavior. Though it may be painful to watch her destroy her life, essentially, it is her choice to keep engaging in such behavior. You cannot change her attitude, but you can change yours. Bear in mind that attitude changes may not be an overnight fix. It may take some time. The point is simple: knowing that you can utilize an attitude adjustment to deal with situations goes a long way when it comes to dealing with hard situations.

Don't waste your time and energy on attempts to change things that are not within your reach. You can't change other people or your past. Make sure you don't spend too much time ruminating over the ways you wish situations or people were different. Accept that things are unfair and difficult at some stage and move forward.

Do you have a plan in place to manage your emotions?

Just because you have reached a place where you can acknowledge a situation for what it is, doesn't mean you will have no emotional connection in the process. It may be hurtful to accept some things. You might be confronted with feelings of anger, sadness or disappointment. Therefore, it would be a wise thing to develop a plan for you to cope with some of your emotions. Ensure that you care for yourself through diet, exercise and adequate sleep. If you have complex feelings, consider journaling or spending time with friends engaging in fun activities like a refreshing outdoor hike. And if you feel really overwhelmed, perhaps it's time to ring up a good therapist or psychologist. There is no harm in pulling in some professional help.

Can you see that only about half of the healing work is recognizing and accepting what goes wrong? The other half is taking action. Get a game plan into place that works for YOU. One of the options you have for any problem is radical acceptance (Hall, 2012). This is about getting to the point where you show no resistance to what can or cannot change and can accept things as they are.

If you have been asking your father to teach you how to fish and he never makes time for you, then you hear that he is going fishing with friends or some colleagues, it may be very hurtful. You may feel rejected and sad. But suffering is what happens when you interpret the pain in negative ways. Pain is often not optional, but suffering is. It's really hard to accept things that we hope are untrue. But the alternative to not accepting things is pain and suffering.

Your trauma is not our fault. You did not ask for the abuse or neglect. You did not deserve any of it. It was all very unfair. You were pretty much collateral damage on someone else's battlefield or an innocent being who was injured out of sheer proximity. Life traumatizes us all in some shape or form. For some of us it happens as awful wrongdoings or other peoples unprocessed feelings and pain.

Regardless the source of our trauma, at some stage in our lives we will be dealt some form of a raw deal.

When this happens you must remember that the event is not your fault. It is just the hand that life dealt. However, the healing and the aftermath of the traumatic incident will always rest upon us. We are responsible for our healing.

My children's drama teacher gave such a great graduation speech really stuck with me. She used the stage and a play as an example of life, where you need to decide if you want to be the hero or the victim. She went on to tell the children that in order for them to not play the victim in life, they need to think differently about getting wounded: *"Children, you must learn the lesson that nature teaches us: we should ask not why we are wounded, but rather how the wound can be healed. And then allow the rest of the story to play out as it is."* I just thought it was the most beautiful thing. I use that principle daily when I work with people on their journey of healing.

Stop and ask not why a wound occurred, because you can't reverse it. But you can ask yourself what you can do to rejuvenate yourself. There is a quote by author D.H. Lawrence that complements the drama teacher's lesson: *"I've never seen a wild thing sorry for itself. A small bird will drop frozen dead from a bough without ever having felt sorry for itself.* Now isn't that just something that nature continuously teaches us? Healing? A tree doesn't ask why the elephant pushed it over. It either regrows or it dies and becomes part of another ecosystem. But it definitely does not feel sorry for itself. So why do we? We must learn to accept our responsibility for our healing."

I urge you to acknowledge that you have been wounded, but to not feel sorry for yourself. Step up and ask how you can heal. I've drafted a healing contract for you to sign. It is a contract making a commitment towards your healing. This is just a rough framework and you can add whatever promises you feel you need to keep to yourself. You can add your own wounds that need special care.

No one knows you better than you do. And if you don't know yourself all that well, as you explore your wounds, you will see how you are actually cracked open in a sense. Only then can you get to know yourself deeper than the surface and realize how natural healing actually comes to us, if we just create a space to allow it.

My Healing Contract

I, _____, understand that I am undertaking a vigorous encounter with my own healing. I commit myself to being patient and kind towards myself during this process. Though the task may seem daunting and triggers immense, though I may feel overwhelmed, heartache and many other fierce emotions, I know that I have everything in me to make it through. I am the primary adult and caregiver in my life.

In everything I have to deal with during this journey, I commit myself to excellent self-care and love through making sure I sleep, eat and exercise well. At times I will allow myself pampering and a gentle response when things get tough.

I promise to myself that I will take responsibility for my healing and that I will let go of the idea that my childhood trauma was my fault. I was an innocent child and I claim my childhood innocence back. I am stepping up for myself in ways my parents or any other parent or caregiver in my life, couldn't.

I am taking the first step towards breaking the cycle of abuse and neglect in my family.

I will keep these small promises to myself during this journey:
_____
_____
_____
_____
_____
_____

_____
Signature

_____
Date

Chapter 2:

My toxic parent

Now that you have accepted the ways in which your childhood traumas and abuse has manifested in your life, we need to direct our conversation away from only understanding ourselves and towards conversing about our relationship with our toxic parent(s). This chapter will explore the forms of toxicity you may have had to endure. We'll be taking a look at the reasons why some parents become toxic and you will be guided into a deeper understanding of your own relationship with our parents and the role he / she / they played directly or indirectly in turning your relationship into a toxic one.

So, What Is A Toxic Parent?

We touched on this in Chapter 1 but in general I feel that the term "toxic parent" is a bit broad with so many definitions. For the purpose of this book, we will consider toxic parents as people who are narcissists, who show emotional immaturity, have substance abuse addictions and who are abusive.

These traits can take on many forms. Let's have a look at some of the most common types of toxic parents (Forward & Buck, C. 1989):

Godlike Parents

This type of parent gives substance to the myth that there are perfect parents. To children, their parents are all-powerful providers. If they need something, their parents supply it. However, young children don't have anything to judge against what their parents provide them with and they just assume that their parents are perfect. When children feel that their parents are ideal, they feel protected. However, when a parent is unpredictable, they become an almost godlike being that a child fears or no longer feels safe in their company. Some parents feel they are automatically entitled to control their children because they were the ones that brought them into this world.

It's tricky when a child is still at the age where they are completely dependent on their parents, since the way in which the child's needs are provided plays a critical role in the child's personality development. As children grow, from around age two, they start to assert their independence. "Normal" parents tolerate this independence as their children learn to explore. They even encourage it. Emotionally healthy and normal parents understand that their children are not an extension of them. They acknowledge that children are developing into autonomous human beings.

On the flip side, you have toxic parents. They tend to have little regard for their children's independence. They see rebellion and any action that asserts the child's own will as an attack on them as a parent. They unconsciously undermine the healthy development of their child, often by reinforcing the child's dependence on them. Children are positioned as helpless without them as "godlike parents" rationalize this action through the belief that they are acting in their child's best interest.

In this sense, toxic parents become godlike to their children -- an unpredictable, strong force that they fear and that needs to be obeyed at all cost. Godlike parents create an environment that often shapes the belief that a child is bad and the parent is good. A child is weak and a parent is strong. These misguided beliefs can long outlive the child's actual physical dependence on their parents.

Remember in Chapter 1, how Karen rationalized that her mother was battering her because she had Karen's best interest at heart? *"My mother only yelled at me or smacked me because she wanted to teach me to have a backbone and not a wishbone. Her intent was obviously not to hurt me."* This also illustrates a classic approach of denial to deal with the truth of a toxic parent. As a child it was too painful to believe that her mother was a tyrant. Instead, Karen perfected the godly parent in her mind and feared her based on her unpredictability and the recurring messaging that her mother was smarter and was acting on her behalf.

The Inadequate Parents

This kind of toxic parent focuses all energies on their own needs for survival. Now, besides children's basic needs to be fed, clothed, homed and protected, they also require additional supports to grow into healthy adults.

Such needs include:

- Emotional nourishment and acknowledgment that the child's feelings are respected. In other words, a child knows that they have a right to not feel the same as their parent(s).
- Children need to be treated in a manner that develops their sense of self-worth.
- Guidelines of appropriate boundaries and limits to the kinds of behavior that is acceptable or unacceptable.
- Permission to make mistakes then be disciplined without physical or emotional abuse.
- The right to be children by being playful, spontaneous and somewhat irresponsible.

When parents are inadequate they have trouble meeting any of the needs above. Healthy, balanced parents give their children chores around the house.

Inadequate parents enforce great responsibility on their children, often at the expense of their innocence and childhood. This usually happens because the parent is incapable of taking good care of themselves (frequently due to depression, lack of social support, neediness, irresponsibility, etc.).

When a child is forced to act like an adult before he or she is an adult, deep emotional scars are often inflicted. Such children fall short because no child can actually function as an adult before they become one. When a parent expects a child to take on major responsibilities, they blur family roles. The result being that a child struggles to emulate, learn from and look up to mature role models. They do not know what responsibilities are assigned to adults and to children.

No child will be able to perform adult duties with the same skill or efficiency as an adult. These shortcomings cause feelings of incompetence and low self-worth in children. Such children are constantly exposed to situations where they feel that they never do good enough. They feel an expectation to make their parents happy in some way for the rest of their lives - no matter how impossible that standard may seem.

In some instances, children of inadequate parents also become overperformers and perfectionists because they constantly feel they should be doing better. Ironically, inadequate parents only focus their energy and behaviors on their own physical and emotional needs to survive and don't pay much attention to their kids. This makes their children feel invisible and it just feeds into a vicious cycle of low self-worth, hidden under a big cloud of overperformance.

The Controllers

Controlling parents experience their children's own identity as a loss, because they see their child as an extension of themselves. Controlling parents operate out of fear of abandonment and a dissatisfaction with the unlived life inside of them. Consequently, they do everything they can to keep their children dependent on them or they control their lives well into adulthood.

They exercise direct control through intimidation that is often humiliating to the child. Controlling parents see their children' feelings as subordinated to their own. This is why children that are raised by these parents tend to be anxious and fearful then struggle to reach maturity. Controlling families function on the premise that a child's opinion has no value and their needs and desires aren't relevant.

Extremely controlling parents even treat their adult children as inadequate and defenseless. They manipulate them into thinking that they constantly need their parents and then they force the grown child into doing things the way the parent prefers.

Two of the controlling parent's "go-to" tools for manipulation is leveraging their children's guilt and shame. They compare their children to other people and themselves, letting them feel inadequate.

Don't forget the constant criticism and leveraging of money to keep their kids dependent and subordinate! Controlling parents will always find a way to make their children feel like they are doing something wrong. When a child is controlled in such an intense and intimidating way that is drenched with guilt, two responses are likely: surrender or rebel. However, in the case of controlling parents, both these reactions imply that you are being controlled even though you are intentionally doing the opposite of what your parents are demanding of you.

The Verbal Abusers

This is one of the most underestimated, underplayed yet damaging forms of abuse. During a recent basic First Aid training course, we were told that the most dangerous wounds are those that you don't see until after an accident. That is why paramedics feel for tenderness and look for discoloration on the surface. If you have internal bleeding and don't get help, an injured person can die within a few minutes while looking fine on the outside. Just because a wound isn't visible doesn't mean that there is no wound or injury. In fact, wounds on the inside are trickier to detect and to treat. I feel the same way when it comes to verbal abuse. Just because a child or person is walking around without bruises doesn't mean that they may not be terribly battered on the inside.

Insulting names, snarky and dismissive comments, along with constant criticism can leave terribly painful emotional scars on their children. Children are left with low self-worth and no personal agency.

Most therapists identify two kinds of verbal abuse:

Direct Style of Verbal Abuse	**Indirect Style of Verbal Abuse**
Parents directly insult their child. They will call them stupid, ugly, worthless, etc. They will directly say to their child that they wish they had never been born.	Parents tend to be: • cynical • narcissistic • sarcastic • tease their kids with a malicious undertone They make "innocent" remarks that hurt just as much as parents who directly verbally abuse their children. Children take sarcasm and teasing at face value. These parents do not know the difference between positive humor and belittling, mean comments.

Verbally abusive parents rationalize their toxic behavior through educational lessons. They will always say that their comments or actions are to make their child a better person or to teach them how to be strong in a hard and cruel world. But children internalize what their parents say and they develop beliefs around it. They have not yet developed to the point where they can distinguish their own beliefs and values from whatever their parents are throwing at them.

People who are very competitive are also more likely to become verbal abusers because they fear that their children will outperform them. This is very similar to what controlling parents do when they push their kids to be the best in everything or excel in careers that they could not achieve or simply did not have the opportunity to achieve.

In both scenarios of controlling and verbally abusive parents, the child's adolescence becomes a huge threat to insecure parents. During this time, the toxic parents may become especially forceful in pushing down and verbally controlling their children to keep them tending to the needs of their parents.

Another form that the verbally abusive parent takes on is that of the *perfectionist parent*. This type of parent is never satisfied with anything their child does. Even the smallest of mistakes become catastrophes. Perfectionist parents do not grasp that making mistakes is a way in which children learn. They impose unreachable goals and expectations on their children and surround them with ever-changing rules. These parents live under the illusion that if their children are perfect, their family will be perfect. However, the opposite is achieved and even more unhappiness is created.

The Physical Abusers

Physical abuse usually occurs due to parents' exhaustion, immense levels of stress, anxiety and their own deep dissatisfactions with their mediocre lives. It is usually accompanied by a side plate of horrible lack of impulse control. Parents who are physical abusers usually come from families where physical abuse was the norm or where they were extremely abused in some other way.

They want their children to meet their needs, like wanting to be served or to be left alone and undisturbed. When these needs are not met - often because a child simply cannot meet them yet - they flip out. The whole explosion is usually a misdirected form of anger. The abusive parent tends to fire the anger they have towards their parents who mistreated them onto their own children. This, however, would be no excuse for their behavior.

When it comes to abusers, it's important to take note of the role of the *passive abuser*. Generally, only one of the two parents physically abuse their children. The other parent does nothing to intervene. They may not even be able to beat a child in any form, but by not doing anything to protect the child from the active abuser, the passive abuser becomes an ally to their partner.

Instead of stepping up and saving a child, the passive parent tends to turn into a frightened child themselves, maybe since they are afraid of the active abuser. The passive parent then acts helplessly instead of rising to their responsibility.

Children are such easy targets for physical abuse because they can't fight back and they are easily silenced through intimidation.

The Alcoholics

Parents who drink heavily engage in all of the above destructive behaviors. Children of alcoholic parents tend to develop a high tolerance for accepting all things unacceptable. When a parent has a drinking problem, they start to develop a "special secret" bond between parent and child. However, this bond is extremely toxic.

Drinking also shatters vulnerability, trust and openness in a family. Alcoholic parents are usually driven by feelings of jealousy, possessiveness and suspicion. Through these relationships, children learn very early on that kinship means betrayal and that love leads to pain.

The Sexual Abusers

Sexual abuse by a parent is one of the ultimate forms of betrayal. Incest is most certainly the most damaging and confusing of human experiences. It's also one of the most difficult forms of abuse to deal with. Incest is any form of physical contact with a child's mouth, breasts, genitals, anus or any other body part, done with the purpose of sexually arousing the aggressor or parent (Forward, S. & Buck, C. 1989). Usually, this includes behavior that has to be kept a secret between the parent and the child.

Dr. Susan Forward (1989) identifies many misconceptions regarding incest in her bestselling book, *Toxic Parents: Overcoming Their Hurtful Legacy and Reclaiming Your Life:*

- It's a rare occurrence.
- It only takes place in poor and uneducated families.
- It's normal for an adult to react in such a way if they are sexually deprived.
- Young girls provoke molestation.
- Sexual abusers are mostly strangers.
- Incest stories are often not true or exaggerated.

Let's get one thing straight here. Parents always have a monopoly when it comes to credibility and power in a family. It doesn't matter how corrupt or toxic they are, they are generally trusted and can cover up incest easily out of sheer positioning as a parent.

Open, loving and communicative families very rarely have cases of incest. That is not because of monetary wealth or education but rather because of their open loving nature. Families that have high levels of emotional isolation, stress, anxiety, secrecy and lack of mutual respect often create an environment where incest rears its nasty head.

The only way a child who falls victim to such a trauma can survive is to construct a psychological cover-up. They basically push the painful memories deep into their unconscious minds. It goes so deep that they may never surface for years, if ever. But the damage of incest is immense. Children who were exposed to incest often feel dirty, different and damaged (sometimes they don't even know why). Humans who are sexually abused are mostly robbed of healthy relationships or sexuality. Many of them become overweight as adults to keep people at a distance because body mass creates an illusion of strength and power.

Why Do Parents Behave This Way?

Each family is a system that consists of a group of interconnected individuals. Each person in this system is affected through and by the system in profound ways. No matter the size of a family, it will always be a complex network of a whole spectrum of positive and negative emotions. Everything is on the table from love, joy and peace to shame, guilt and anxiety. Families have a constant flow of a wide range of human emotions that are all connected to some need, value or belief.

However, not a lot is immediately visible at first glance of any family. One has to go beyond the surface to see what the family rules, beliefs and emotional drivers are. Attitudes and judgments in a family are driven by hidden/unspoken roles and underlying beliefs. You can often pick up on these rules if you listen to what the families describe with the words "should," "supposed to" and "ought." On a more direct level, these beliefs can also be communicated through the "dos" and "don'ts" in the family.

In most reasonably mature and healthy families, underlying beliefs are formed in a way that is considerate towards all feelings and needs of the various family members. Rules are reasonable and serve as an ethical and moral code to the development of children in the family.

When it comes to toxic families, unwritten rules and beliefs are self-centered and stand in service of the toxic parent(s). Rules will be grounded in bizarre or distorted versions of reality. This uncertainty and inconsistency puts children in a vulnerable place where they can easily be abused.

It's important to realize that your parents also had parents. When it comes to toxic families, you basically have a domino effect. One generation tips over into the next. Essentially, the family system you grew up in is not one that your parents invented. It is the accumulation of feelings, rules, events and beliefs that have been passed down through generations. In other words, your parents' behavior or toxicity has most likely been in the family for generations. They did not change into toxic monsters overnight. They were raised into them by toxic or immature parents. One can only parent to the level of awareness one has at that specific moment in time. If your parents don't know any better, why would they actually want to "do better?" Chances are great that they are unaware of what they are actually inflicting on their children because their behavior has never been corrected or adapted.

In an average well-functioning family, most parents will cope with life challenges by communicating about their problems and working them through. Together, they explore solutions or options to handle what life throws at them. They are not afraid to seek help if they need to. On the flip side, toxic parents only react when it comes to problems. They tend to act out their fears and frustration under pressure and do not take into account what consequences their actions may have on their children.

These are some ways in which toxic parents try to cope with problems (Forward, S. & Buck, C., 1989):

1. *Denial*
   They pretend that nothing is wrong. If something does go wrong, they convince themselves it won't happen again. They also minimize, rationalize and make jokes to relabel their destructive behavior. They constantly hide problems behind euphemisms.
2. *Projection*
   Parents accuse their children of the very shortcomings they have themselves. For example, if a mother can't keep her job, she will accuse her children of being lazy and ambitionless. Or they blame the child for their toxic behavior. In a similar example, a mother will blame her children for causing her to be too tired to go to work and be efficient, saying it's their fault that she is constantly losing her jobs. Projection is also often used to help the parent dodge responsibility for their own behavior.
3. *Sabotage*
   This may sound crazy and counterintuitive, but in families where a parent is very dysfunctional (drunk, ill, extremely violent, etc.), other family members tend to take on the roles of rescuers. This creates a kind of balance that is quite comfy. But when the dysfunctional parent starts to heal or go into a proper treatment plan, you'll be surprised at how often the rest of the family may unconsciously find ways to sabotage their progress. This tends to be especially true for the co-parent of the dysfunctional parent, because they do not want the constructed balance to be

disturbed. Toxic parents even sometimes revoke therapy for their children once the child starts to rebound. The latter very strongly links to controlling and inadequate parents' behavior. I once worked with a physically disabled girl whose father was addicted to painkillers. He would use his daughter's medical condition to get his hands on prescription drugs. His wife was addicted to alcohol, but went into rehab. He seduced her back into drinking because her sobriety made her notice how he was getting his hands on prescription meds.

4. *Triangling*

Family systems that are toxic will often have one parent who sides with a child as their confidant or ally against the other parent. In such a case, the child is enveloped in an unhealthy triangle where they are pulled apart and feel they need to choose a side. I experienced this, especially after my parents divorced. My mother would command me to call my father and tell him that she needs more money for my upkeep. My father would tell me how she was misusing that money for her leisurely lifestyle, that she needed to adjust her spending and create her own income. This made me feel like a burden and also guilty because I felt I was the cause of their financial distress and arguments. Triangling effectively turns a child into a dumping ground for the parents' emotional baggage. The toxic parents gain a little relief from their discomfort without having to confront their issues as mature adults.

5. *Keeping secrets*
Toxic parents just love keeping secrets. It allows them the opportunity to fragment their families into little "packs" where no outsiders are allowed in. Although the family pack is fragmented "inside," to the outside world it's "us against them." The feeling of guarding secrets together unites the family. Think about a child who hides physical abuse by telling the teacher that she fell down the stairs. Her lie is protecting the family pack from outside disturbances. The child does not yet know how damaging the secret actually is. He or she is just after the acceptance and praise they can garner for guarding the family's little secret.

From a perspective where families are complex systems passed down through generations, do you now understand that a lot of your parents' (and even your own) self-destructive behavior comes from the obedience to twisted and warped rules? There are forces much more powerful that drive your parent's behavior and even your own.

If you get this, you're just another big step closer to change. Soon, you will be able to see new options and choices for yourself and generations to come. However, to see things differently is not enough. Real change and freedom can only come when you reach a point where you are empowered enough to start *doing* things differently.

Types of Child Abuse

Up until now, we've had a thorough look at the type of toxic parents that exist and why they behave the way they do. Let's now closely examine the actual behavior: the different ways in which children can be abused.

There really are many awful examples, but for the purpose of this book we will mostly be focusing on *emotional abuse, mental abuse* and *neglect*.

It's important to recognize that emotional abuse can also come with physical, sexual, financial, abuse, etc. You might have picked some of this up when we looked at the different types of toxic parents and their tactics.

Leading mental-health influencer and award-winning author, Christine Hammond, identifies seven types of parental abuse in one of her leading articles on PsychCentral (2017). We will explore these so you will become aware of the many forms of physical, emotional and mental abuse.

I've put them in the form of a table so you can review it as a list to see if you have experienced any of these forms of abuse or if you can identify these in your family or close friends' families.

Type of Abuse	Children abused in this manner have experienced:

Physical	*Intimidation* Parent standing over a child or getting in their face without backing off (even if the child requests it). *Isolation* Parent ensures that the child has limited options to escape a dangerous situation or their temper. *Restraint* Child is confined to a space due to the parent restraining them. This can be done through blocking a doorway or even tying a child up. *Aggression* Slapping, hitting, punishing, biting, burning, stabbing, shaking, pinching, strangling, force feeding, choking, etc. Any hurtful or forceful behavior. *Endangerment* A parent verbally threatens a child with murder and other violent acts, even with weapons.

Mental	*Rage* Sudden outbursts of immense anger that seem to come from nowhere and are often directed at the child. These acts shock them into silence or compliance. *Gaslighting* Parent intentionally lies or reshapes past events so that the child will doubt their memory and sanity. *Intense Stares* Subjecting the child to an emotionless face, often for long periods of time. *Silent Treatment* Child is ignored for extended periods in order to punish them. *Projection* Parent simply dumps a problem onto their child and accuses the child of being responsible. *Twisting The Truth* When parent is confronted for their actions, they make it seem like their

behavior or an incident was the child's fault.

Manipulation

Making a child fear something bad, like abandonment or rejection, in order for the parent to get something they want.

The Victim Card

As a last resort, the parent often plays the victim to ensure that the child's behavior remains under their control.

Verbal	*Extreme Changes in Volume and Tone of Voice* Parent suddenly yells, screams or switches to silence and ignores their child, refusing to respond to them or acknowledge them. *Intimidating Words* Parent uses swear words and threats when a child is not acting according to their will. *Intense Forms of Speech* The manner in which the parent speaks turns demanding and argumentative. They talk over their children and interrogate them. *Personal Attacks* Can take various forms like criticizing, mocking, teasing, uttering judgmental opinions and character defamation. *No Apologies* There is a refusal to take responsibility for their actions from the parents' side. They become very hostile when a child asks about promises and commitments, for example. They will never apologize

	for wrongful actions against their children.
	Blame
	Any problem or thing that goes wrong is blamed on the child. Often the child will be made out as being too sensitive or overreactive.

Emotional	*Nitpicking* The parent belittles anything the child does and makes anything that is important to the child, inferior to the agenda of the parent. Teasing or sarcasm is often used to degrade the child and then when the child is upset, they are made out as too sensitive or ridiculous. *Shame* A parent will share personal or private information that exposes their child in a shameful light. For example, proclaiming that the child wet his or her bed again. Child is constantly reminded of their shortcomings. *Increased Levels of Anxiety* When a child is constantly interrogated about every move or never know what their inconsistent parent will do next, they become anxious very easily. *Guilt* Parents condition their children to believe that they should be the most important thing in their life. Anything that defies that belief is twisted in ways

to make the child feel guilty for not treating the parent as the center of the child's universe.

Insecurity

Children are held to unreachable and unrealistic standards that set them up for failure. When the child does fail, they are made out as useless or inferior.

Confusion

Children are seen as extensions of their parents in terms of boundaries and roles, not seen as separate humans. The child does not know where they end and the parent starts and vice versa.

Alienation

Children are told that other friends and family members are unimportant so that the parent can position themselves at the center of the child's life.

Anger and Fear

Parents generate anger in their children when they intimidate them, threaten them or display behavior that scares the child. Just think of all the anger Karen (from the story in Chapter 1) experienced due to her mother's intimidating behavior. She was scared of her but also angry at her mother for many years.

Rejection

Parents reject their children's affection and deny their worth in order to make the child feel like love is being withheld from them. This way the parent can manipulate the child in doing what they want them to do. If they don't, they withhold love so the child will listen to them and feel like they won't be rejected.

Financial	*Forbidden Access* Children are not allowed to access their money or possessions that they were gifted. *Stealing* Child is exploited and defrauded and stolen from. *Assets* Parent demands that any inheritances or financially valuable gifts be placed in the parent's name. In some instances, the parent also opens bank accounts in the child's name. *Bills / Credit Cards* Accounts are put in the child's name without their knowledge. *Unrealistic Budgets* A child is put on a budget so strict that it is impossible to follow. Children get demotivated when they cannot keep to the unrealistic expectation that just sets them up for failure. *Spending*

| | Parent controls a child's spending to the point where they may be punished if they spend their own money.

Career

It's forbidden for the child to earn money or receive an education as this tends to be seen as something that gives them independence and threatens the child's dependency on the parent. |
|---|---|

Sexual	*Grooming* Intentional embarrassing (or unwanted) sexual act with a child where the goal is to catch the child off-guard and make them feel anxious or dreadful. *Molestation* Unwelcome touching of private bodily parts, either by the child or the parent. *Sexual Exposure* The act of making a child look at their parent's genitals or private areas as the parent engages in a sexual act. *Threatened With Abuse* Child is threatened with the possibility of abusing someone else in order to bully the child into doing sexual acts. *Inciting Fear* Child gives in to unwanted sexual acts out fear that the parent will hurt, humiliate or abandon them. *Destroying Principles*

Next level of sexual grooming involves making the child watch pornography together.

Rape

Penetration of the vagina or anus - with any body part, object, orally or by a sex organ of another - without the consent of the victim.

Sadistic Sex

This can go as far as the parent drugging the child, making them drunk, administering pain during sexual acts, physical beatings, choking, cutting and even murder before, during or after sex.

Spiritual	*Divided Thinking* The parent conditions the child into a place where there are only two kinds of people: people who agree with the parent and ones who don't. Parents tend to mock or belittle anyone else who does not agree with them. *Elitism* Parents do not allow contact with anyone they consider impure or unholy. *Submission* The child is made to believe that they have to wholly adopt their parent's point of view. A parent's authority may not be questioned. *Labeling* The child is made to believe that people who do not align or adhere to their parents' beliefs are demonic, enemies of faith, disobedient and has inferior value. *Public Performance* Perfection and happiness is expected at all times. Religious activities like attending church is demanded and

rigid. The child needs to appear "picture perfect" and appropriate at all times.

Legalistic

The parents' rules and regulations are the governing law in the life of the child with absolute statements about small things like hair color, clothing or jewelry.

Segregation

Friends or family outside of the religion are shunned or alienated.

Blind Obedience

The Child is expected to always submit to the parent and basically worship them. No questions asked.

Abuse of Authority

Parents misuse their spiritual authority to justify their children's submission to them.

Fraud

In some cases, parents commit a criminal offense and cover it up in the name of their religion. This can include hiding all the aforementioned types of

	abuse by somehow rationalizing or justifying it with their religion.

See how many forms abuse can take on, especially when it comes to the parent-child relationship? Be mindful and vigilant of this kind of behavior. In my own journey of healing, once I understood how subtle some of the ways abusive behavior can be, I wondered: Is it possible that abuse is hereditary? Or is it purely learned from generation to generation?

Is Abuse Biologically Hereditary?

Earlier in this chapter, we investigated some of the reasons why abusive parents behave the way that they do. We came to the conclusion that families are complex systems that are embedded with hidden beliefs and rules that have been passed on through generations. After all, parents were also once children and they probably also have suffered unresolved trauma and abuse. Simply put: there is no simple answer to explain why some parents or adults abuse children. The elements that lead to abuse are interwoven with many other complex issues. The more complex the issues, the harder it is to understand the abuse itself.

Now here's a little something interesting I would like to share with you. Though most abusive behavior is learned between generations, I recently came upon a study that suggests that childhood abuse may be transmitted through DNA and may in fact be biologically hereditary.

There are many behavioral mechanisms through which trauma can negatively impact the next generation. Child abuse is another possible way. According to a Harvard University study, childhood abuse can leave marks that are seared deeper than just psychological trauma; the trauma actually etched itself to the research participant's DNA. The research was based on a small sample of men and showed that there were differences in chemical marks within the genetic code of participants that experienced abuse in childhood.

A chemical process called methylation helped scientists examine sperm samples. Noticeable differences were evident in the samples of victims and non-victims. These findings suggest a long-term physical impact of trauma. The presence of these changes in sperm cells suggest that the legacy of childhood trauma may actually be passed between generations. This research is still in its infancy, however there is tangible evidence of "molecular scars" indicating that DNA seems to be physically impacted by traumatic childhood experiences.

The further impact of these changes are still largely mysterious in humans. But the study also refers to experiments on mice that indicated that when sperm cells are altered through methylation, health problems could be transmitted to their offspring. Some of the findings of the mouse study showed that early-life stressors affected their sperm and, in turn, those altered sperm cells affected the health of their offspring by specifically creating a form of anxious behavior.

In the sample of 34 men (that were all part of a long-term study by Harvard's TH Chan School of Public Health), it was found that 22 men were victims of some form of child abuse. In the samples taken from these men, 12 areas of DNA were consistently struck by a degree of methylation in the child-abuse victims. If this effect were to be seen in larger studies consistently, scientists reckon that the process could be applied in legal settings. How? The methylation of DNA can be a potentially useful resource for criminal investigations. Essentially this study shows that the correlation between methylation and child abuse may provide a percentage of probability that abuse had occurred (Gabbatiss, 2018).

Crazy isn't it? Look, don't get me wrong, I don't believe that every man who was abused as a child will produce abusive offspring. This study is too shallow and doesn't say much for any impact on genetics in women. What I did take from this study is how really deep our trauma can manifest. Scientists discover so many new things daily. Who knows how deeply childhood trauma can actually be embedded in us? The point is there is some science pointing to some form of hereditary nature of child abuse. But primarily, abuse is passed on through toxic family systems in many different ways. All we can do is accept that we are part of the system. We can accept that trauma will happen to us at some stage in our lives. We can accept that our parents' trauma was likely bestowed upon them from previous generations. And we can accept the responsibility to heal ourselves and take the first step in breaking the generational cycle of abuse.

So what now?

Now we summarize a few key thoughts in this chapter and look at ways you can recognize if you are leaning towards showing any traits of becoming an abuser yourself. I know, that's not a nice thought. But remember, awareness is the first step to acceptance. And beyond acceptance is where the healing lies.

By now it should also be clear that many abusers perceive their behavior as normal or acceptable because that is what they learned as children. I'm not suggesting every person who was abused as a child will become an abuser, but if you really want to break the cycle of abuse and toxic parenting in your generation, you'll have to do some deep introspection - just in case. We are all humans and we all have certain blind spots. Keep in mind that if you perhaps do find some of these behaviors present in your life, it's not the end of the world. You are just taking a step into the end of that world as you knew it. Change is scary. Our egos will resist it. Humans don't like getting out of their comfort zone.

Be honest, kind and patient with yourself as we go to work and become more and more aware of how our toxic parents or abuse may rear its head in our lives and relationships.

Main ways how toxicity is handed down:

I just want to clear something up. In this book, we refer to toxic people. It's just a practical way of phrasing the concept and how society refers to people who display destructive behavior towards themselves and others. However, I just want to take a moment to reflect on this: there is no such thing as toxic people, but rather people who engage in toxic behavior. So let's have a look at some of the ways that toxic behavior may have been handed down on you.

If there is a slight hint of toxicity in you, just remember that you have toxic traits in you, but you are not essentially toxic. You will also very likely start out by becoming your own abuser then potentially the abuser of others. Your parents did not invent your toxic family environment. It has been the result of a whole bunch of accumulated emotions, beliefs, rules and interactions that has been passed down in your family.

Here are some of the main ways toxic family systems are passed on from one generation to the next (Forward & Buck, 1989):

- *Repetition Compulsion*
  Humans are drawn to things that are familiar to us. Regardless of the fact that those things may be bad, if it is familiar, it provides a sense of comfort. Familiarity gives a feeling of structure because we think we know what to expect of it and feel less at risk. We do not like change nor do we like uncertainty. When we know rules, we know what to expect. In toxic relationships, if the rule is bad, it doesn't really matter to the child because to them it remains a rule and they know what to expect if it is disobeyed. This is also why the relationship patterns with people close to us tend to be the same as the ones we learned in the relationship with our parents. We anticipate that other people will behave towards us in the same way our parents did. In fact, we expect it of them. Put differently, in our adulthood, we tend to seek intimate relationships similar to the ones we had with our parents. And this is how we get caught in repetitive cycles of toxic relationships.

- *Rage Outlets*
  One of the common characteristics of kids who were raised by toxic parents is that they often express rage. It is an accumulated build-up due

to the oppression from their parents after not being allowed to express how they really feel. One simply cannot be battered and humiliated and not feel some form of anger. Due to the fact that a child doesn't have a way of expressing their anger, he/she will carry it inside them until they can find an outlet in adulthood. This outlet often comes in the form of violent behavior, criminal activity, manipulation (all external outlets) or depression, illness, muscle stiffness or headaches (internal outlets). If you recognize any of these in your adult life, stop and consider whether your rage may be coming from anger you've been carrying towards your parents, as this is another way in which toxicity is transferred between generations.

- *Abused to Abuser*
  In some instances, a child makes the assumption that if they were to adapt the same qualities as their abusive parent, they would be protected in some way. When children are victimized, they tend to fantasize how they could protect themselves by means of acting like their abuser. This way they end up developing the same damaging traits as their toxic parents.

With all this in mind, you don't have to excuse your parents for their behavior. But again, we get closer to a deeper understanding of how toxic behavior functions. Next, we are able to position you as the person who will take the first steps in discontinuing the toxic behavior with your children and other close relationships.

Things to Recognize on The Path to Healing

As we've established earlier, toxic families have unspoken rules and beliefs that make their children vulnerable to abuse.

Be on the lookout for any of these beliefs in your life:

- Children must always respect their parents, without exception. Even if they do something wrong or immoral, you have been made to believe that they must be respected purely because of their title or position as a parent.
- The only way to do things is your parents' way.
- Children should be seen but not heard.
- You are not allowed to be mad or angry at your parents.

Here are some examples of unspoken rules in a toxic family:

- You may not be more successful than your parents.
- You may never lead your own life.
- You may never stop needing your parents.

- You may never be happier than your parents.

If you recognize any of these examples in your own family or relationship with your parents, it's okay. As a child you were most likely conditioned into obeying these rules and adapting these beliefs because children blindly obey toxic or abusive family rules to avoid punishment. Further to that, children do not want to be seen as a traitor to the family by not abiding by the rules, no matter how horrible the child's position may be due to their obedience to twisted rules.

But there is great hope ahead. These rules have been made up. Constructed. And they can be reconstructed. None of the toxic behavior in your life has to be permanent.

However, life isn't always fair and pain is a part of life. You will get hurt at some stage and no one can take care of you but yourself. Only you can feel where it really hurts. You may need some help tending to some wounds, but ultimately, you are the person who does the after care after a big operation. You need to redress the wounds. You need to do the rehabilitation exercises so that you may have optimum use of the part of you that was wounded.

Sometimes our wounds are even so bad that we never gain full mobility back from the parts that were broken. But they still heal. We are made for renewal. We are naturally geared to heal. You literally have new hair and nails growing weekly. You shed old skin. New ones grow. After a sunburn, you peel and then you glow again. But it all takes time and loving kindness towards yourself.

When trauma strikes, your response (no matter what) is NORMAL, when an event is ABNORMAL. You have everything in you that you need to not just survive, but thrive. It is just going to take some time and hard work. The healing journey is not an easy one. It is not without pain. But there is no better time to start your healing journey but now.

Two of the most important words you will learn to make your own during your healing journey will be: *"Let go."* See, contrary to popular belief that we need to "hang in there," I think it is harder but more rewarding to "let go." That means we need to let go of a space we know. Sometimes the spaces or environments we are used to aren't healthy or safe, but it's all we know so we are not willing to release that space and seek something different. As humans, we are much more inclined to just stay where we are.

Just like in Chapter 1, we prefer the "status quo." We so easily get stuck in a set of mind that intermittent reinforcement of the things we desire is enough. That somehow, little bits of what we want now and then, is enough to sustain us. Do you want to be sustained or overflowing? Do you want to feel abundant love? Then why do we keep settling for less? As an abused child, for example, you may have been used to only receiving crumbs of love, approval and support. The result is that, as you grew older, you were satisfied with the occasional scrap of any of those things you need.

In addition to this, we are also inclined to see losses as "near wins." When your dismissive mother sounds mildly interested in your day, you hope that she will finally see and acknowledge your existence as her child. Your father pays you a compliment and you hope that he will realize that you are not a weakling or inadequate in his eyes. Be careful in your healing that you do not put on your rose-tinted glasses and see things for something it isn't. You will just set yourself up for disappointment. In some cases people are so toxic that the best thing you can do is accept it and put some distance between yourself and them.

Also be mindful of ruminating thoughts. Women tend to be more vulnerable to this pitfall. Abused children sometimes grow up to be adults who can stay focused on hurtful situations from the past and the present. Where they keep replaying history in their minds and make up all kinds of versions where they see how they could or should have done things differently. In these ruminative thoughts they keep second-guessing themselves instead of just acting on the thought by addressing and accepting what they need to and then move along.

Okay, we also need to just stop to look at what "letting go" is not. It definitely is not denial or pretending that the past did not happen, that you were left unscarred or untraumatized by toxic behavior. You do not have to let your parents off the hook without claiming responsibility for their misconduct. It rather focuses on the ability to distinguish between ways of thinking that keep you stuck and feeling overwhelmed. You should be able to identify thought processes that will assist you in moving on with your life and subsequent healing.

One of the ways in which you can help yourself distinguish between these thought patterns is called goal disengagement (Streep, 2018). This is essentially a four-step process:

- *Cognitive disengagement* involves letting go of the thoughts that maintain your "status quo." This requires the skill to stop ruminating on a goal you set but did not achieve. Continuous worry about "what if" scenarios could point you in a direction where you will probably convince yourself that you shouldn't let go after all. Thoughts like: "What if I leave and my mom overdoses if I don't check up on her? Her death will be my fault."

- *Affective disengagement* is a step that manages the emotions that are involved in letting go or "quitting on" toxic people or habits. This asks you to process the emotions that surface when you fail to achieve what you set out to do, whether it's feeling guilty, useless or just a loop of blaming yourself. You must let them surface and let them go. If your parent, for example, has to face some form of harsh consequence and you made it your goal to protect them (due to their manipulative nature), you must let the guilt surface. Then acknowledge that it was not your fault. They are a person in their own right. He/

She was the adult. You were the child. Now you are an adult. And you are working towards becoming a mature adult. If your parent remains an immature and insecure adult, that's on him/her. You do not have to allow your parent's toxic behavior in your life as an adult. Your relationship has changed from *adult-to-child* to *adult-to-adult*. Remember that. If you have toxic people in your life, you must let them go for at least 90 days. Heal yourself, disengage from any conversation or interaction with them. Make them respect you and your time. You are an adult and the issues they bring to the table are not your responsibility. If you are being supported by them financially, do not accept anything from them. This is how they are controlling you. If you feel obligated to help them remember this: "You can not help anyone unless you heal yourself first."

- *Motivational disengagement* is letting go of a previous goal, such as giving up on the way you want your parents to acknowledge you or stopping them from turning to substance abuse again. In this step you need to start considering and planning a new goal for yourself. Do *you* want to have a healthy family? Do you want to buy a car *you* like? Do *you* want to get more active and join hiking clubs? Do *you* want to make more friends or go to the church of *your* choice? Decide on what you want and need, not what your parents want or need on your behalf.

Here is where you start to identify some boundaries; you do not have to be an extension of your parents. You are a wonderful human being in your own right.

- *Behavioral disengagement* involves putting new plans into action for a new goal, such as loving yourself and giving to yourself what your parents couldn't give to you. Now you act on what you've planned. Keep small daily promises to yourself and gradually your future will change.

You also need to be aware that there is a core conflict when it comes to motivational and behavioral disengagement (Streep, 2018). This conflict refers to the tension between you acknowledging that you need to manage your relationship with your parents and family of origin and that you also have a continuing need for parental attention, love and support.

We tend to struggle to find balance between putting boundaries into place that keep us healthy as adults in our own right while acknowledging that we have an inner child that will always seek love and affection from our parents. This conflict usually keeps us in the status quo.

We need to make the difficult decisions and have a clear game plan for boundary implementation or else we will just go back to the status quo or default scenario. As long as we don't clear up the core conflict in our motivational disengagement process, acting differently in behavioral disengagement is impossible.

Strategies to Get Unstuck

If you find yourself stuck and unable to let go, here are some strategies to help you get free. This is also the point in the book where I want you to start shifting your focus away from what your parents did to you and onto what you can start doing for yourself.

Going forward, as I share more strategies in the book, I would like to make it clear that this book by no means intends to replace a good therapist or psychologist. This is hard and sensitive work. Depending on the areas you struggle with, it might be good to use this book as enhancement while joining a Twelve Step program or support group. Some readers may be equipped and choose to do this work on your own. That's brave. But if you are an adult who was victim to physical and sexual abuse as a child, I would really recommend that you seek some professional help in conjunction with this book.

I'll share a little more about my personal story in the next chapter, but I can tell you that I would definitely not be able to work through my trauma alone. I had, no I *have,* the most wonderful psychologist with whom

I've been working since the beginning of my journey in that hipster coffee shop with that little life quote. I still see her every now and then to align and check in with myself. Make sure any bad habits or doubts don't return. Again, this is a process you commit to over a lifetime.

Now, here are some strategies to keep yourself committed to the changes you need to implement your healing journey. Status quo, off you go!

1. *Recognize and remind yourself that it's not your fault.*
   Once you realize that you are not at blame, it makes way for you to realize that you cannot fix everything on your own. Your parents have to co-operate and take responsibility for their role in your life. If they don't, you are allowed to move on and outgrow them. Remember, your relationship is adult-to-adult now.

2. *Abusive and toxic behavior should not be normalized.*
   As children, we normalize the behavior that we are surrounded by and often we continue this behavior as adults. As you grow, you may get to know other people who have a different reality: one of love, balance and maturity. You are allowed to choose how you want to be treated. Do you want love, safety and balance? Then don't allow cruel behavior in your midst. It

does not have to be your "normal."

3. *Boundaries for the wins!*
   If you want to cultivate a new mindset, you will have to carve out mental space to figure out how you will manage your relationship with your parents going forward. You are allowed to cut things out and limit contact. Do whatever you need to so you can have space for clear thinking. You are allowed to figure out where they stop and you start.

4. *Expand your emotional skill set.*
   You will have to make work of exploring every emotion you experience. Name them. Look at them deeply and explore where they originated, especially when you think about your relationship with your parents. See if you can identify the guilt from shame. Find out what negative feelings you have about yourself that may have manifested due to hidden beliefs from childhood.

5. *Manage Your Thoughts.*
   I love comparing useless actions with a rocking chair! Rumination and worry keep you busy, just like a rocking chart, but they really bring you nowhere. If you struggle with replays in your thoughts, instead of fighting them and counterintuitively make the worry even worse, schedule a time for yourself where you can worry. In that time, allow yourself to think out

the worst-case scenarios then draw up a chart or list of options you have to deal with these scenarios. This will do wonders for calming your subconscious thoughts.

Letting go is a skill that is invaluable and within your reach. Just start with small steps.

Reflection

Chapter 2 was quite a bulky chapter, so let's just reflect on a few key thoughts before we head on over to the next sections.

- *"I'm addicted to you. Don't you know that you're toxic?"* Whoa! I remember dancing to that Britney Spears song at university parties. However, you do not have to dance to the toxic tune of your parents. The first step is to acknowledge that you had toxic parents or childhood abuse in your life.

- After acknowledging that, work on understanding and defining your particular situation. Remember families are complex systems. Dysfunctional family systems each differ in terms of a complex network of a whole spectrum of positive and negative feelings.

- In toxic families, there are underlying beliefs and unwritten rules that are almost always self-centered in favor of the parent(s).

- Due to the fact that children are not familiar with any other frame of reference outside of their family, they consider everything that they learn within this system to be a fundamental or universal truth.

- A family system without personal freedom is a toxic system. As a rule, unhealthy families discourage individual expression. Hence, you need to take the time to study your toxic parent based on the seven types of toxic parents we discussed.

- After identifying your type of toxic parent, you need to make an effort to educate yourself about the manners in which your toxic parents behave. Once you are familiar with how their behavior was toxic, you will come to learn how it may have affected your life and caused some distorted perspectives in your life.

- When you are able to identify the problems they caused, you will be better equipped to examine your own wounds and get your strategies for healing in place. If you understand the toxic behavior of your parents and what possibly caused it, you may be in a better position to manage your relationship with your toxic parent.

- We also looked at the different kinds of parental abuse you could face, along with pitfalls to navigate past so you don't continue the cycle of abuse. The abused usually becomes the abuser. Very often, we abuse ourselves then others.

- We learned that there are four steps to "letting go" on our path to healing. There are strategies we can put into place to make sure we don't stay stuck in the status quo, due to conflicting thoughts regarding our relationship with our parents.

- Lastly, we always need to remember that trauma was not our fault, but that we are responsible for our own healing.

Healing is amplified when we are in a safe space, so in the next chapter we'll be looking at how we can create our own.

Chapter 3:

A Safe Space For Healing

When a soldier is wounded on the battleground, he is moved to safety before anyone tends to his wounds. The same accounts for our emotional battles. If we have been hurt, we need to get to a safe space where our wounds are assessed and treated until we can get to a hospital or safe place where the real healing can happen.

In the previous chapters, we have had an in-depth look at our relationship (with ourselves and parents) and the conversation between ourselves and the world. There is still a big question that lingers: *"When do I actually start feeling better?"* Chapter 3 will explore the idea that the second and most crucial step towards healing (after understanding) is to have a space safe enough to allow internal movement to happen. Here we will relocate ourselves from the emotional battleground into a haven where we can assess our wounds, treat them and start feeling better.

Recognizing the traumatic experience is one of the toughest jobs you have to do. Not only will you be confronted with your past but it also might trigger in you an increase of the symptoms of that trauma. It's like pouring surgical alcohol on an open painful wound. Washing the wound clean ignites a lot of pain, but in the end, it gets better and you are guarded from future infection.

Safe Space

What is it?

The term "safe space" has several definitions. It can refer to a space where dialogues are open and free of judgment (with others and with yourself). It can be a space where you can be honest with yourself without fear. Or it can be a space that is physically protected from any sort of threat, like discrimination or violence.

Why do I need it?

You cannot truly start a healing process if you feel vulnerable and exposed to a wide range of uncomfortable thoughts and emotions. Much like on a battleground, if you have gaping wounds and are still in the scope of danger, a bomb can drop, you can be shot down again or you may get dirt or infections in your wounds. If we try to recover in the midst of a battle, the chances of healing are slim. You are also using all your energy just to survive and not on thinking clearly what your different injuries need. All you know is you need to get out alive.

Only once we are safe, we can really look at what treatment is different for each wound. You need to be able to go through the experience in your mind in a detached way. The only way to do that is by feeling safe.

How do I create it?

A feeling of safety and security is essential for emotional and physical well-being. There are two ways in which you can create a safe space for yourself: mentally and physically.

Mentally
Mentally you can create a safe space through exercises like art, visualization and mindfulness.

Using your imagination to create a safe space to visit can be a great de-stressor and very calming for people who struggle with anxiety or who have been traumatized. If something triggers you, you can engage your imagination to internally go to your safe place as a means to soothe and self-regulate.

You can create your imaginary safe place through journaling, guided imagery exercises and conversation. However, incorporating art into this exercise can lend great depth to the experience. The visual, experiential aspects of making art can help a person to see their safe space realized before them, through their own hands. They literally get in touch with a feeling of safety and security as they paint or draw their haven through the medium of their choice.

Art therapist and psychotherapist, Carolyn Mehlomakulu, explains on her 2017 blog post, that some clients feel adverse to guided imagery and meditation and are simply more comfortable engaging in art. Additionally, some clients just can't seem to relate to feelings of safety due to the extent of their trauma, but found the starting point to just relate via art as less intimidating and very calming. They already seem better just by creating art. Mehlomakulu (2017) also notes that children in particular find the ongoing reminder, once the artwork of their safe place is finished, helpful.

I also participated in art therapy (in combination with hypnosis), but here's what I found so precious: to create your safe space in front of your eyes is a peaceful act. I was soothed from imagining the picture that I would paint, by simply choosing the colors. Oh, then there's the wonderful feeling of making the decisions and being in charge of what your safe place will look like. I chose my safe space based on a real-life place where I actually felt safe for the first time in years.

After living in a big city with my husband and two young kids, I felt numb at times. During that period, I was attacked in my car with a knife held against my throat. It was enough to push me to make a first drastic change. I needed to feel something besides nothing, before my whole life went by "unlived." I took my kids out of school for a year and rented a cottage against a mountain. My husband joined us for a few weeks each month.

In that year, I took the time to find myself. For the first time (perhaps ever), I could really breathe and take the time to look at the trees around me, some of which were hundreds of years old. By feeling the life-force and wisdom contained within them I started to feel the life-force and wisdom contained within me. I had space and time to reflect on what I was feeling inside. That cottage, surrounded by all those majestic trees, is where I go in my mind when I feel overwhelmed. That mountain cottage was a tough and sudden change from my busy city life but it was a saving grace. It was the place where I took up the challenge to step up and heal myself.

"In creating a safe place we can go beyond simply trying to connect with a past emotional experience by painting a memory. We move beyond the idea of expecting that our eternal reality must be a certain way for us to feel safe and relaxed. Instead, we are harnessing our mind's power to create an inner sense of peace, safety or relaxation regardless of the circumstances around us." (Mehlomakulu, 2017)

However, if art really isn't your thing, here are 10 steps you can follow to create a safe space in your mind:

1. Find somewhere comfortable and make sure you can remain there for 15 to 20 minutes without interruptions. It's a good idea to sit in a chair that supports your back and allows you to plant your feet firmly on the floor. Then close your eyes once comfortable or place the focus of your gaze at something that is pleasant. Keep your focus there.

2. Take slow breaths. Breathe in for 5 seconds and exhale for 5 seconds. Continue for a while until your body relaxes then bring your attention inwards.

3. Choose a place where you feel safe and create that image in your mind. Identify a place in nature or any location that brings you joy and peace. You can also make a picture up of where you want to go one day. If you're super imaginative, you can even create your own fantasy land or planet - just for you. For some active people, that space can even be watching yourself running or doing yoga. The idea is for your body to associate with a place where it can feel calm and safe.

4. Describe to yourself in detail what you see in your safe space. How does it look? Are there trees, water or rocks? What are the colors that surround you? Are there other people there?

5. Describe the sensations in your body when you are in that space. Is there a breeze on your skin? Perhaps you feel cool water at your feet.

6. What smells are providing comfort or calm? Is there some smell of food cooking? Freshly cut grass?

7. Are there sounds or silence in your safe space?

8. Once you have taken enough time to create a detailed picture and sensations, plot yourself in the scene. What are you doing? Sitting? Lying down on some soft grass? Are you walking? Swimming? What are you wearing?

9. Now take a mental snapshot of yourself in that space.

10. Lastly, you need to develop a cue, word or phrase that represents this space to you. Use the word that describes the place to you and say the word while you imagine that space over and over. Repeat it at least 5 times. Effectively, you will tell your mind to associate with that word and when you cue yourself, you will be able to "go" there in a matter of seconds. If you feel unsettled, use the word to evoke the memory of your safe place. At times, I found that the word often wasn't a strong enough cue for me. My therapist suggested I link a small bodily gesture to it. I press my middle fingers

> against my thumbs and say "my porch." I immediately feel the breeze and that little touch grounds me when my thoughts feel a little scattered. If you do not have a reference to a safe place like I did, you can use the simple, yet effective phrase: "I am worthy to live this life and I will keep myself safe and sane."

Once you have established your safe place and cues, you need to bring your attention back to the present moment and your current surroundings. Do this gently and patiently.

It helps to reinforce your cues daily. Take 10 to 15 minutes in your day to "go there" until you are able to transport yourself quickly and on cue, when you need calm.

Physically

You can also physically create a safe space around you by cutting ties with toxic people and behaviors, but I'm not going to get into that immediately. We actually have the whole next chapter dedicated to how to break ties with toxic parents. So stay tuned and, in the meantime, just note that safe spaces can be created mentally and physically.

If you're in the position that you are still living with the parent, you can do things like getting a key to lock your bedroom door so you can have a toxin-free space, even if your parent doesn't like it. You are a person in your own right and you are allowed to create a safe space for yourself.

Empathy vs. Sympathy

Emotionally, there is also an important distinction to make to help you to create distance for an emotionally safe space. We often use empathy and sympathy as synonyms.

For the purpose of this book we consider empathy as more important than sympathy. Renowned researcher-storyteller and Ted Talk guru, Dr. Brené Brown is one of the thought leaders when it comes to differentiating between empathy and sympathy. Brown (2013) argues that empathy fuels connection and sympathy drives disconnection, because empathy is a skill that can be developed within yourself to make people feel included. Sympathy on the other hand creates an uneven power dynamic because it is almost a form of pity which can often lead to isolation and disconnection. Brown states that empathy requires of us to recall or reflect on the feelings that make us feel uncomfortable. When you practice empathy, you are acknowledging and working with feelings like frustration, nervousness and confusion. Then you actually take those perspectives and try to relate with others with those perspectives in mind. Brown argues that empathy is a very vulnerable choice.

According to Brown (2013), empathy means taking someone else's perspective and putting yourself in other's shoes. while in that position you need to listen without judging them. You also need to open yourself to feeling and recognizing a feeling that you notice in them, that you have felt before and can relate to. Lastly you need to actually communicate that you recognize that emotion in the person with whom you are practicing empathy.

Between Brown's perspectives on empathy and my own healing journey, I've formulated four basic steps to create self-empathy. Remember earlier when I said that we often start to abuse ourselves? Well, I believe empathy towards ourselves, along with a little compassion, can go a long way in preventing ourselves from beating ourselves up.

4 Steps to Self-Empathy

1. *Acknowledge yourself as a being with feelings.* You are not an inanimate object or a robot. You are wired to feel things. You are made up of sensations. We smell, we see, we taste, we have such amazing senses and that all plays together into what makes us feel alive. Our feelings protect us but they can also overwhelm us.

    Often when we are busy or when a feeling is not necessarily a pleasant one, we just ignore or dismiss it. However, if we numb one feeling, we basically numb all our feelings. But they will never go away completely because it's part of our human nature. We very easily suppress our feelings in service of the goals we pursue, but to practice empathy with ourselves, we need to stop and acknowledge that it is okay to feel a range of emotions.

2. *Say hello to your deepest needs.*
Once you have allowed yourself to acknowledge your feelings, you must admit to yourself that deep down you just want to be happy and avoid any form of suffering. There is nothing wrong with that. To not want to suffer is one of our most primal instincts. Our feelings actually developed to help us survive against threats. But they don't always just keep threats at a distance, they also draw us closer to the things our hearts desire. But again, numb one feeling, you numb them all. In order to have empathy with yourself, you need to allow yourself to be sensitive to your emotional needs. Sometimes we don't want to acknowledge what we need and desire because we're afraid we won't get it. If there is no expectation, there will be no disappointment. Allow yourself to feel what you need and listen to your inner self.

3. *You must grasp that life is not easy.*
Suffering is all around us. No one in this world will ever go without suffering. When you suffer, you are not failing. Life is happening. Empathy can sometimes mean that you need to tell

yourself that you are doing something challenging by just being a human. When you are having a difficult time, you are being human and basically you've been set up for hardship through your evolutionary past. But you need to just be kind and courageous when it comes to yourself and your journey.

4. *You have to have your own back.*
   My therapist once shared this quote with me. It basically comes down to the fact that you need to be kind to everyone you meet because you don't know what battle they are fighting. Now my question is: Who do you meet most often? Yourself, of course. You wake up with yourself. You walk with yourself. You go to bed with yourself. Are you being kind to yourself upon every encounter? Do you support yourself and have your own back?

Once you have created a safe space, mentally, physically and emotionally, you must recognize the symptoms of your past trauma that still linger in adult life, within that safe space.

Now you can start to generate an awareness of where your problems lie and allow yourself space and time to adopt the proper tools to deal with them.

Importance of Self-Regulation

Once you are in your safe space and gradually start to face your problems and get the tools in place to start dealing with them, it is important to learn how to self-regulate your emotions. Through self-regulation you can distance yourself from your emotions (without numbing them) and feel safe while dealing with your trauma. Always remember that no matter how agitated or anxious you can get, you can always take a moment to change your arousal system and calm yourself. Your safe place is a way to self-regulate, but there are also other ways to relieve some of the anxiety associated with trauma. Once you start to get more experienced in practicing self-regulation you will also generate a greater sense of control.

Tips to practice self-regulation:

- Anchor yourself through sensory focus. Take in what you see, hear and also what people are around you. As you become more present in the moment, you realize that you are safe and there is no threat.

- Connect with what's going on inside. You can do this by noticing what you feel inside of you. Recognize your gifts, wisdom, natural intelligence, strength and the resilience you have to adapt to change.

- Practice mindful breathing when you feel disoriented, confused or upset. It is a quick and effective way to calm yourself. Simply take 60 breaths and stay focused on each exhalation.

- It's also a good idea to have a safety reference. Just think about the "safe place" artwork we spoke about earlier. That artwork is a great example of a safety reference.

  But it doesn't only have to be an object, it may also be a nice memory, or a person, etc.

Additional Tips for Recovering From Trauma:

- *Get moving!*
  Trauma disrupts your body's natural balance and puts your body in a state of hyperarousal and fear. In this state, you have a lot of adrenaline and endorphins rushing through your body. Exercise can help your nervous system recover and repair itself.

  Try to at least get in 30 minutes of exercise daily. Try something that engages arms and legs like dancing, running, swimming, etc. Then throw in a little mindfulness as an extra treat. What do I mean by this? Try to keep your thoughts inside your body. Feel what your body feels as you exercise. Notice sensations like your feet hitting the floor when you run or the feeling of the water rushing over your body when you swim.

- *Make sure you don't isolate yourself completely.*
  After you go through a traumatic experience, you may want to withdraw from others but that's really not a great idea. When you connect to other people, it helps your healing. Just make sure you connect with people who release good energy your way. Alone time is good, but too much can be horrible for someone who has been traumatized. When you do connect with people, you don't have to talk about the trauma. Talk about other things that make you feel engaged.

  You may also ask for support. Put yourself in the shoes of your supporters who didn't go through the same trauma you did. They want to be there for you but they don't know what to say or do. Sometimes one of the kindest things you can do for yourself and the people who care about you is to tell them how they can support you and ask them to do so.

  Make a point of taking part in social activities even if you don't feel like it. To do "normal" things with people helps you to disengage from the trauma that has been overshadowing your life. To reconnect with old friends may also be a good idea if you retreated from them, especially if those relationships were important and valuable to you.

- *Health is wealth!*
  If you have a healthy body, you can increase your capability to cope with trauma.
  So make sure you get plenty of sleep, avoid alcohol and drugs, eat a well-balanced diet and make sure you reduce any stress factors in your life as much as possible. Think about it, in essence, a healthy body in itself is also a kind of safe space.

That brings us to the end of this chapter where we focused on the importance of creating a safe haven for your healing. This chapter spoke mostly to the ways we can create mentally and emotionally safe spaces. We mentioned that we can also create physical safe spaces, but as promised, we'll get a little deeper into that in our next chapter on when one should consider cutting ties with your toxic parents.

Chapter 4:

To cut or not to cut the ties?

Sometimes creating a safe space is just not enough. In order to process trauma, one needs to be able to take some distance from what triggers it. When trying to heal from childhood abuse caused by a parent, one can choose to cut the ties and create some healthy boundaries that will help the healing process. But you can also choose to try to fix it first. This chapter will help you to assess your situation and give you some insight into what to do if you are considering the tough decision of removing your toxic parent from your life.

Now that you've built an awareness, an understanding and some form of acceptance of the situation, it's time to go deep into yourself and start figuring out what you need to heal. Now that you're an adult, you also have more options and choices!

It's okay to cut the ties with your parents:

Look, no one is perfect. But there does come a point where our parents' flaws can just become downright destructive and can take away children's right to love and nurture. When kids are raised on a diet of toxic behavior, it's usually only a matter of time before they take over from their parents. Sometimes they lash out towards themselves and other times their own children or the people within relationships that resemble their family systems.

Now we've pretty thoroughly discussed the ways in which to create a safe space for healing mentally. But what do we do when a mental space alone just doesn't cut it anymore?

It is an extremely difficult decision to consider letting a toxic parent go. But on the flip side, it could also be one of the most important decisions of your life. As humans, we are wired to connect with the people who deserve our trust. But as disease or infection can spread in our physical bodies, so can toxic parenting consume our lives with their infectious nature. Sometimes, to stop it from spreading through your whole body, you need to amputate. Sometimes love is not enough. People can get broken to the point will only keep damaging you.

You are allowed to choose your own healing over their continuous self-destruction. You are not by any means responsible for the state of their relationships or their healing. You do not have to stand in line and wait for the next form of abuse, belittlement or shaming. Cutting anyone out of your life is hard and it's even harder when it is your parent. But sometimes the relationship is just too toxic, so amputating or divorcing the pattern is the best option. But how do you even start such a process?

For your own peace of mind, you might want to ask yourself the following to decide whether you need to cut ties or not:

- Do you feel like you have tried everything else and they seem to just continue in exactly the same manner?
- Do you feel constantly emotionally exhausted, like you can't go on when you are with them?
- Do you often hear people around you tell you that they can see how much you are hurting because of your parent's influence and behavior?

It is imperative that if you choose to go through with it that:

You're practicing some form of self-love
If you are dealing with a toxic parent to the extent where you need to let them go and cut them out of your life, it's my honest opinion that you get some therapy before, during and after the event. If you

speak to someone who is impartial, you may get peace of mind after rationally discussing the decision. Other than that, yoga, meditation and journaling can be a great way to envelop yourself in mindfulness. This will help you to take mental and emotional inventory of how you are actually coping throughout the process. Though you are creating a physical boundary, it will be the hardest work to keep a mental boundary in places where you do not allow the toxic parent to occupy space in your thoughts where they can still impact your life.

You have a good support system
You need to know that you are not alone. When you let your toxic parent go - however counterintuitive this may sound - you may feel a sense of guilt and abandonment. They emotionally abandoned you as a child and now you are physically and emotionally abandoning them too. But this is where you need support from folks who can keep you in line with the right perspectives.

The big difference is that you were a child back then and they were adults. Now you are both adults. And they are still an immature adult where you are working on your growth and levels of maturity... They did not show up for you but now you are showing up for yourself. Support groups or getting into some group therapy can be really great for this. If you live in a place with limited access to such groups, with a little Google search, you should be able to find an online support group that may also help.

Don't allow yourself to be isolated. You are definitely not the first or only person who had to make this call. Once you get to know people who are in a similar situation, you may learn new insights and recognize some common patterns of toxic parents. This in itself will provide a sense of validation for such a tough decision.

Let the guilt go
With such a tough decision, there is bound to be some feelings of guilt and shame. You will have to prepare yourself to let them go. In most cases, the parent you will be divorcing is the person who raised you - and however limited the means were - provided for you to some extent. But this is where you have to remind yourself that you can have gratitude for what they gave you, while maintaining your boundaries.

You do not have to feel like you *owe* your parents your time and attention. Your parent(s) chose to bring you into this world and it was their responsibility to provide and raise you in a healthy way. Even though your relationship changes from child-parent to adult-adult, the roles still remain: they are the parent and you are their child. If reconciliation is possible, the parent has to initiate or in the least co-operate. It is not your responsibility to hang around if they continue their abusive and destructive behavior.

You're clear about your intentions
You have to do a little soul searching and make sure your intention is healing for yourself. Don't make a

decision like this out of spite. This should be about instilling firm boundaries so you can move on with your life. This is not a battle act or manipulative maneuver.

Anger and hurt will surface with these kinds of issues but you cannot allow unprocessed pain and emotions steer this decision.

It's also okay if you don't cut the ties:

Don't be too hard on yourself if you do decide to not step away right now. If you do decide to return to an abusive relationship, chances are that you might fall into a pit of self-loathing. You may ask yourself why you weren't strong enough to break free. Loyalty is always an admirable trait. It is just in this case a trait that got in your way of saving yourself.

Take a moment to own where you are and just give yourself permission to be in that space. If you keep breaking yourself down, you will never build up enough love for yourself to be able to change your expectations for yourself. In a sense, it really does take huge amounts of strength to walk back into a relationship where you know you will get hurt. Give yourself time.

You will know when you are truly ready. But for now, rest assured that that is enough. That is okay.

Now if you are going to stay, you could consider these options to better equip yourself to manage possible future conflict between yourself and your parents.

- Try to understand your parent's story. And asked them to fully explain their behaviors. Even if you disagree, it will give you perspective as to why your parents engage in certain behaviors and the rationale behind it. If you fully understand each other, you may find some safe middle ground.

- Consider seeking the advice of another adult. If you know for a fact your parents are not going to give you great pearls of wisdom, it may be a great gift to yourself if you befriend another adult who has similar values and love, rather than fighting with your flesh and blood for love they have never fully given you.

- Since you returned to the relationship, it would be wise to clarify what you want from conversations or conflict when you do still see them. Do you want an apology? To prove you were right? Whatever it is that you want answered, you need to make sure you have set realistic rules and goals for yourself to reach. You may not always get the perfect apology. Rather, focus on long-term goals that will work towards keeping the relationship steady with as little tension as possible. In the short term, you may get an apology but not acknowledgement.

- Refrain from name-calling and "playing psychologist"

- Let go of the need to make your parents understand.

- Make sure you are calm first

- Always approach them without haste, in calm and from a place of love.

- Using simple words that don't overcomplicate things

- Be as honest as possible.

- Frequently ask yourself if you are breathing deeply.

- Are you calm enough to actually have this conversation?

Setting healthy boundaries

Healthy boundaries help you focus on staying mentally and emotionally stable.

How to Set Healthy Boundaries

Boundaries are an important part of establishing our identities. They are also critical for our well-being. Boundaries can be physical or emotional. They can range from loose or very rigid. Healthy boundaries fall somewhere in between these two poles.

These limits between you and another person create clear indications or markings of where the one person ends and you begin - and vice versa. The main purpose of boundaries is to protect you (Selva, 2020). But healthy boundaries should be consistent and ensure that you are mentally and emotionally stable. If we have no boundaries, we struggle with defining our identity. They can be either psychological, emotional or physical. Physical boundaries may sound like: "I appreciate a hug, but I prefer if you ask me first" or "I don't mind if you sit next to me on the couch, I just don't want you to put your arm around me." It is just a way to communicate what is okay in your world and what is not.

Boundaries not only protect you but they also guide people who engage with you on what behavior is appropriate or inappropriate for your well-being. Emotional or psychological boundaries may sound something like this: "I love that you want to come over and visit. I just don't appreciate it when you show up unannounced every time."

Benefits of Healthy Boundaries

Boundaries can be helpful in many ways:
- They can build a stronger self-esteem because you make yourself a priority. People trust that people who can take care of themselves will be able to take care of others. Boundaries make us feel safe and build trust.
- They help you to conserve emotional energy because if you do not protect yourself from the demands of the world, you may develop resentment towards others because you cannot stand up for yourself. Just because you are willing to help your parents with a task does not mean you have to be happy to do some emotional lifting through the drama they create with their toxic behavior.
- Boundaries enable us to safely grow and be vulnerable. Our emotions are often complex but we can protect ourselves to keep our fragile parts safe. When we are strong enough to let a

boundary down, we show our vulnerability. Examples include having a difficult conversation with your parents and being able to speak your heart without being afraid of the response. If we allow ourselves to be vulnerable, we communicate to the people around us that they can also open up to us. However, when you have toxic parents, it is important that you differentiate between oversharing and being vulnerable. When vulnerability is shared, people grow closer over time. But oversharing can take on the form of drama that manipulates and holds other people emotionally hostage.

Tips on Building and Preserving Your Boundaries

Boundaries are a crucial ingredient for healthy relationships. Remember how abused children tend to view themselves as an extension of their parents? Furthermore, victims of sexual abuse at a young age also have physical and emotional boundary issues. As you grow older, learn how to set new boundaries as an adult because it wasn't taught to you.

- Learn to express your limits. You need to know where you stand on a matter if you want to enforce a boundary.
- You will have to learn to listen to your feelings. If you feel discomfort or resentment towards

someone, chances are very likely that you do not have a healthy enough boundary in place.
- Some people easily understand the maintenance of healthy boundaries. But many don't. When you communicate your boundaries, it's important that you be direct in your approach when it comes to people who may have different personality types or different generational backgrounds, etc. Sometimes, people don't respect your boundaries just because they do not understand them or find them unclear.

Boundaries and Consequences

It is one thing to set boundaries, but what happens when they are crossed? You must decide on the consequences if that happens. The best consequences follow naturally from the other person's actions. For example, what if your toxic parent rings you up every day just to fight because you don't phone them every day? If they keep phoning to fight, you may say to them that the consequence is that you will not answer or if you answer and they fight, you will hang up without continuing the conversation.

Common Tactics of Manipulative Parents

Manipulative parent will always push boundaries. Don't fall for their traps. Here are some common tactics devious parents implement (Flint, 2019):

1. They will make *personal attacks* on their children to diminish their self-esteem and gain psychological control over them. They may blame their kids for other family problems, bring up past mistakes or tell the child that they are not good enough to be a part of the family. You do not have to believe those lies or allow them to bring you down.

2. They will *invalidate your feelings* and make you feel that your emotions are worthless. Manipulative parents may interrupt their kids, act like they know their feelings or thoughts then try to change how a child feels about situations.

3. If things aren't going your parent's way, they will *withdraw love* from you. They may do this by avoiding to look at you or refusing to touch you.

Releasing attachment to the outcome creates space for you to remain at peace, regardless of how the unknown unfolds.

Writing Exercise: Pros and Cons of Cutting Ties

It might help to write out a pros and cons list. Write out all the benefits of getting distance with your parents versus any disadvantages you can think of. You might include pros such as "Peace of mind," while cons might be "Missing their presence."

Should I Cut Ties With My Parents?	
Pros	**Cons**

Chapter 5: Oh, my feelings!

Now you have created a safe space and set some boundaries. You know where your parents stop and where you start. By now you should be a little more resilient and courageous. Are you willing to face your inner fears and demons? In this chapter, we explore the most common emotions that childhood trauma causes and ways to truly deal with them in the healthiest manner.

No healing comes without acceptance: first, of one's own situation, the hurt, the fact that one cannot change their parents and all the emotions that stemmed from dealing with trauma and abuse. Only then can those be changed. Hence, in order to heal we must validate and process our emotions. We must allow ourselves access to the feelings that we were not allowed to feel growing up. Anger, fear, shame, sadness, resentment and grief are among them.

Check in with yourself in order to identify your lingering emotions.

Below is a list of emotional words to help you broaden your emotional vocabulary.

Amazed

Angry

Annoyed

Anxious

Ashamed

Bitter

Bored

Comfortable

Confused

Content

Depressed

Determined

Disdain

Disgusted

Eager

Embarrassed

Energetic

Excited

Foolish

Frustrated

Furious

Grieving

Happy

Hopeful

Hurt

Inadequate

Insecure

Inspired

Irritated

Jealous

Joyous

Lonely

Lost

Loving

Miserable

Nervous

Overwhelmed

Peaceful

Proud

Relieved

Resentful

Sad

Satisfied

Self-conscious

Shocked

Silly

Stupid

Suspicious

Tense

Terrified

Trapped

Uncomfortable

Worried

Worthless

This list is quite extensive so let's narrow down some of the most common types of emotional reactions to abuse: *Self-blame, guilt and shame*. But also *Anger, Sadness and Grief*.

The last three main emotions will be discussed.

Self-Blame

Self-blame is not always a bad thing. Feeling responsibility, guilt or shame keeps us from hurting others and lets us learn from our mistakes. It helps us be more empathetic towards each other.

Child-abuse survivors try to try to understand why trauma occurred to them and diminish the sense of uncontrollability of the world. However, it appears that trauma survivors have the tendency to believe that they brought the trauma upon themselves.

The toxic parent has a way of transferring blame and guilt to their children. They do this by taking something private or personal that happened to the child, then share it in a shameful, public way. A kid who accidentally wet his or her bed will be exposed and mocked in front of people who came to visit the next day. Children will also be constantly reminded of their shortcomings, often in a passive-aggressive way.

Furthermore, toxic parents feel entitled to be the most important person in the life of their child. Then they make the child feel guilty for not giving them all their attention. They will often blame the child for being hurt.

Self-blame has also been called the ultimate emotional abuse (Formica, 2013). Some say it is the most toxic form of emotional abuse because it enhances our perceived inadequacies. Whether the blame is real or imagined, it does have to have the power to paralyze us.

In order for us to release feelings of self-blame, we have to recognize the responsibilities of the people involved. Who has to take a stance? Once the person responsible has been identified, that person has to step up and be accountable for their actions.

How to deal with self-blame:

Humans need a sense of stability in which they construct their lives. There is an inner need to feel that the world has some kind of order and balance. But when a child is a trauma survivor, he or she usually thinks that they are "bad." When a child blames themself, it is a way in which they feel in control. To feel mastery helps to reduce anxiety that a trauma will reoccur. People who react to trauma with self-blame give themselves a misguided sense of power.

Here are some brief ideas to explore in managing your self-blame:

- Realize you are good enough, even with your flaws. You do not have to be perfect to be loved.
- Repeat after me: "Everything is not my fault."
- Make a point in your life to distinguish between taking responsibility and self-blame. Taking responsibility is holding *yourself* accountable for *your* actions; self-blame is taking on the responsibility of the world.
- Don't reduce yourself to your imperfections or faults. You are so much more valuable than your output.
- Develop self-compassion.

- Learn to identify guilt and shame because they are the direct result of self-blame.

Shame vs. Guilt

Shame is hard to talk about. Everyone tends to have a visceral response to the word. Shame does not discriminate. It is a universal emotion: everyone has it but no one wants to talk about it. Shame is the deeply painful feeling that we are flawed and, therefore, unworthy of receiving love, connection and belonging. Shame is very different from guilt. Shame is a focus on the self whereas guilt is a focus on behavior. Shame says: "I am bad." Guilt says: "I did something bad." (Brown, 2020).

Does any of this sound familiar? Let's take an example. Say you came home as a child after you did not do very well on a test. Your toxic parent sees the result and tells you that you are stupid. For that child, self-blame and shame-talk will become the default setting when confronted with a flaw. They will immediately tell themselves (just as their toxic parent has been drilling into them) that they are stupid or dumb. This may continue well into adulthood.

However, what we need to learn is to focus on guilt in such situations. A guilty response would have been something like "I'm not stupid. I did not study enough because I was tending to my abusive parent's needs all evening." Or perhaps the child was beaten and too distraught to study. The point remains that abused children will have immense levels of self-blame and, consequently, shame and guilt. As an adult, you can now distinguish between the fact that you are not bad or stupid. You can do bad or stupid things.

If you focus on behavior instead of self, you are much more likely to respond with empathy and will be able change your behavior over time.

Anger

Anger is usually a central theme in a survivor's response to trauma because it is a core element of the survival response in humans. It helps us cope by providing us with increased energy to get over our obstacles. However, when anger gets out of hand, it can often cause a total loss of self-control and can lead to problems in your personal life. In addition to this, people tend to use anger to get their way or make their victims submit to their authority. In a sort of invisible agreement between aggressor and victim, a victim submits to their aggressor's demands or threats, effectively enabling and reinforcing the behavior of the aggressor. In the same way the victim is also enabled and reinforced: submission lightens stress levels and halts the aggression. This "agreement" can create space for a long-term abusive relationship. Look to the example of an authoritarian parent who demands that their older child take care of a younger sibling. The parent is relieved of their responsibility towards raising the younger child, and feels in control when the older child submits to the command. The older child feels relief when the parent backs off when he / she looks after their younger sibling. The older child may even feel "special" and trustworthy for being handed such a responsibility. But in reality, the parent is burdening their eldest. Yet both parties get a misguided sense of reinforcement out of the dominant-submissive relationship.

How can post-traumatic anger become a problem:

There are three elements of post-traumatic anger that can turn maladaptive with a person's ability to adjust to "normal" situations that don't involve an extreme threat:

- *Arousal*
  When in a state of anger, our bodies become hyper-activated. Our heart rate goes up; our glandular systems cook up a bunch of hormones and chemical messengers, while our brain works overtime to regulate what our bodies need and it is processing what is going on around us. Sometimes when people experience post-traumatic stress disorder (PTSD), this hyper-activated internal state

becomes their "normal state." They are basically permanently living on the edge and may be irritable or easily provoked. In this state, they will either keep seeking situations where they can stay alert and ward off potential threats. This is where they constantly pick fights to get rid of the anger and this constant edgy feeling. Alternatively, they turn to drugs or alcohol to numb or reduce the internal tension.

- *Behavior*
  People who were extremely traumatized at a young age will usually learn one way of reacting when threatened. Most often this would be an aggressive reaction. Behavioral aggression may take the form of combativeness towards other people, passive-aggressiveness (like deliberately completing a task poorly, sabotaging or complaining etc.) or self-aggression (like self-destructive behavior, chronically harsh self-talk, self-injury, etc.).

- *Thoughts and beliefs*
  When we've been traumatized, the thoughts and beliefs we made up in that moment can actually be exaggerated or warped. For example, a child with one parent that denies the other parent's alcohol addiction, may grow into an adult with the fundamental belief that their own reality cannot be trusted. If a parent constantly criticizes their child about their

body, the child will grow up believing that his / her body is something to be shameful about and will likely want to be "invisible" in order not to attract attention to their body.

If you note any of these three components, you may be more traumatized than you think. PTSD is tricky and getting some professional guidance on your specific traumatic experiences, and the manifestation of your anger, may be strongly advisable.

How to express anger in a healthy way:

It's no secret that people who suffer from PTSD often experience anger. It is actually considered one of the disorder's hyperarousal symptoms (Tull, 2020). In order to better manage your anger, work on distinguishing between constructive and destructive anger.

Constructive Anger
This is not as strong as destructive anger and it can be healed. It is a type of rage that can be managed but, to do so, you will have to know your own needs as well as others'. You will have to approach your anger and listen to what it communicates to you.

For example if your inconsistent parent phones and cancels dinner with you at the last minute, communicate that you are angry about the last-minute change of plans. Then suggest ways that you can work together to prevent future instances like this. Set a boundary and communicate that if it happens again, you will no longer make dinner appointments unless they come to you, for example. In this way, anger is used to take constructive control over the situation while maintaining your self-respect.

Destructive Anger

Destructive anger is a means of expressing anger that causes harm. It may include aggressive behavior (like mentioned in the previous section). It also tends to be a stronger emotion that lasts longer and surfaces frequently. If you do not tend to your anger, it will keep piling up and grow until the point where it will explode.

In a sense, destructive anger can work on a short-term basis to release tension, but the immediate short-term expression of anger may have long-term negative consequences.

Let's take the same example of the dinner scenario. Perhaps you yelled at your parents, cut them off, called them names or even, in an extreme moment, drove to their home just to yell at them. That may provide an immediate release of frustration. However, your parents may retaliate and punish you in a long-term way if they were, for example, still being abusive or manipulative towards you as an adult. Alternatively, you could also turn to substance abuse to numb the anger, which in itself has a range of future problems.

Anger is not an easy or simple emotion to deal with, especially when it is related to PTSD. But you can learn to listen and get to know your anger, its sources and its triggers. Then work on your responses as you get to know it. If you understand why your anger is surfacing, it makes you feel less unpredictable and overwhelming.

Anger Management: Practical Tips:

If you struggle with anger, consider some of these tips to keep your mind off it.

- Keep a journal.
- Find a hobby.
- Exercise daily. A mere 30 minutes a day will do!
- Practice self-love. This is very important and we'll get into it in the next chapter.
- Acknowledge your anger and don't deny it. It needs management, not dismissal.
- Talk about the hurt in your life, either to close friends or members of an organized support group.

Sadness And Grief

We don't often speak about grief or loss in this perspective, especially if our parents are still alive. But

I'm going to let you in on a valuable secret: we must grieve the loss of the ideal parent we never had and are never going to have.

You will need time to recognize and accept your parent's limited capacity to show love because something was broken inside of him or her a long time ago.

Grief And Its Stages

When you mourn the loss of the ideal parent you wanted, it's' almost like going through a break-up. You probably fought very hard to hold on to the relationship and tried to "fix" your parents. Or you kept hoping they would step up and raise you the way you deserve to be raised. By now, we've come to accept that we cannot change our parents. We are not responsible for their behaviors, so now we can say goodbye to that picture in our minds of a perfect, loving parent. This "letting go" can be a very emotional process because it feels like a great loss.

Here are some stages you may experience as you work through your grief. They don't always follow chronologically, however. You may even experience them all at once or in a different order during your process.

1. You will be *desperate for answers*. Why did this happen? Who's to blame? What did you do

wrong? You'll probably talk to friends and fixate a little on these kinds of questions. You'll eventually make peace with the fact that you may never know the answers.
2. *Denial.* You feel like this can't be happening and postpone your grief because it may just be too painful to face.
3. *Bargaining.* You start to negotiate with yourself that maybe your parents will change. Perhaps you are giving up too soon. You promise to be better for your parents. No matter how much you want to, you cannot take responsibility for everything. You know this deep down. Give yourself time to accept that.
4. *Relapse.* It may get so painful to deal with your loss that you may actually return to your parents and try to go back to how things were. You will find yourself standing in line for more neglect and abuse. Unfortunately, you may need to bump your head again so you can see things through as the reality of the loss sinks in.
5. *Anger.* You will reach a point of anger. Anger at the situation. Perhaps yourself or at your parents for not stepping up and "losing you" while they are still alive. This is normal. You may just want to connect to the anger in a constructive way like we discussed earlier in this chapter.
6. *Initial Acceptance.* This is a kind of acceptance that can feel more like surrender. Know you have to let go, even though you may not really want to or feel ready.

7. *Redirected Hope.* Initially, all your hope of love and acceptance was placed on your parents. Hoping they would step up, see you, etc. But now you can start redirecting your hope to other places. You can hope for a life with less drama. You can know that you will show up for yourself even if the adults who did not show up for you, still don't do so. You are not dependent on them anymore.

Only after grieving will we be able to really release and move on. Also, remember it is equally important to share that grief with your support system. Grieving is a very important part of the healing process and we should give it the time and space it needs.

Important Things To Grieve

Sometimes, it's almost like we don't know what we are actually grieving, but we still feel sad. If you struggle to pinpoint what you are actually grieving about when it comes to a toxic parent, here are a few bullet points to help clear things up or give you some vocabulary on what you are feeling.

You are grieving:

- The love you lost (that may not even have been given to you from the start).
- The ideal parent that never was and never will be.

- A childhood that never was.
- That you were robbed of your innocence, in a sense.
- The memories that will not be made with your parents.
- The loss of the future that will not be experienced in the same way as it would have been if you had a loving and supportive parent.

There may be other emotions experienced as a result of abuse and trauma. One of the best ways to deal with those is to cultivate self-love. And what are the tools for self-love? Stay tuned for lessons on how to adopt this life-changing outlook.

Chapter 6:

A self-loving you

Dealing with trauma-induced emotions won't be complete without embracing the act of self-love. By now, you have made a lot of progress and you may even start to feel like the shackles from your past are loosening up.

I remember when I reached this point of *relief*, the perspective that it was not all my fault and that I did not have to carry all the responsibility of bad things that happened to me. My therapist asked me: "So what now?"

"What do you mean *'what now?'*" I replied. "You're supposed to be guiding me into the next steps."

"So what are you going to do now that you have nothing left to blame your pain on?" she said.

Those words hit hard. I had no clue what I was going to do. I had so many options, so many points of reference. Everything I thought I knew and believed had changed. I could not rely on my crippling beliefs anymore. I also knew I did not want to fall back in my old patterns. I had to find a whole new way of treating myself.

This is probably the point where you should also start to craft a new way in which you treat yourself. This is what this chapter is all about. You can create a better alternative for your life that you never even dared to venture into. From now on, you will walk through life intentionally seeking self-loving behavior.

Dissecting Limiting Beliefs

The first step is to examine beliefs that hold you back. Before you can move forward, you will have to listen to the way you speak your limiting beliefs to yourself. Then you need to change the way you talk to yourself. A great way to do this is to use more positive affirmations and tell your inner critic to calm down and take a break. You are now in loving control.

We so easily focus on negative thoughts. I personally found that I started speaking more nicely to myself through affirmations I repeat, than trying to combat my negative self-talk. As I started focusing on the affirmations, the negative language just started having less space in my mind.

- Write out your affirmations. Identify the things you want manifested and the new beliefs you want to instill in your life.
- Make sure your affirmations are statements that you speak, as if they already are that way.

I have flaws but I am still worthy of love.
It is okay to make mistakes.
I can always try this again.
You can also make statements about the words that describe your inner being.
I am funny.
My story matters.
People like to be around me.
I am intelligent.
The more affirmations you have, the more weapons you have in your artillery to fight off the negative self-talk.
- To write these down once is not enough. Your negative beliefs have been repeated throughout your whole life until now. You must repeat them to yourself daily.

Hey, Little One: Reconnecting With Your Inner Child

Who Is My Inner Child?

The Inner Child is a psychological reality. Everyone was once a child and we still have that person inside us but as adults we are less aware of it. We seldom consciously relate to this inner child and that disconnect is often where a lot of our behavioral and emotional relationship struggles are rooted (Diamond, 2008).

All children age. Some of them grow and age into mature adults. Some people reach adult age, but not maturity.

"To become adults, we've been taught that our inner child -- representing our child-like capacity for innocence, wonder, awe, joy, sensitivity and playfulness -- must be stifled, quarantined or even killed. The inner child comprises and potentiates these positive qualities. But it also holds our accumulated childhood hurts, traumas, fears and angers. "Grown-ups" are convinced they have successfully outgrown, jettisoned and left this child -- and its emotional baggage -- long behind. But this is far from the truth." (Diamond, 2008).

This quote by psychiatrist, Dr. Stephen Diamond, clearly illustrates the importance of connecting with our inner child. It is only by loving and healing our inner child can we begin to love ourselves and thereafter, others.

Steps To Connect With Your Inner Child:

Try these simple prompts to get in touch with your inner child:

1. Formulate a dialogue with him or her while alone. See if you can sense them.
2. Consider writing a letter to him or her, if talking out loud with yourself feels silly.
3. Say nurturing things to the child. (I love you. I hear you. Thank you. I'm sorry.)
4. Look at photos of yourself as a child.
5. Think or write about what you loved doing when you were a child. Do you still like those things? Try engaging in them to see if they create a childlike excitement in you.
6. Engage in meditation and creative visualization with your inner child.

How do I Know if my Inner Child is Wounded?

Once you've connected with the inner child, you may find that the child is distant. Here are some signs that your inner child may be wounded:

- You have a general feeling that something is wrong with you deep down.
- You are described as a people-pleaser.
- You struggle to find a strong sense of identity.
- You tend to be a hoarder of things, people and emotions. You struggle to let things go.
- You experience a feeling of inadequacy in your role as a man or a woman.
- Commitment and trust are foreign things to you.

- Deep abandonment issues surface in your relationships and you are inclined to become clingy.

If you identify wounds, one of the best things to do is to practice self-love and, from there, pour that love onto your inner child when you practice the steps of connecting with him or her.

Here's a quick guide on how to get started on indulging yourself in self-love.

Indulging in Self-Love

Self-love is the greatest gift you can give yourself. But before we continue, just a quick note: it is important not to confuse self-love and selfishness.

Self-love allows you to fill the gaps that external sources of love may leave. Only you will ever know exactly how and where you need to be loved. You know your inner workings best and once you connect that to some self-love; you will find the alignment will help you to make healthier choices in life.

Self-love is particularly important when it comes to setting boundaries in your relationship with a parent or parents. Once you have a clear understanding of what your boundaries are, have put them in place and have communicated them, you show that you value yourself.

The Four components of Self-love:

In his book *The Art of Loving* (1957), author Erich Fromm, identifies four components of self-love.

Self-Care

Fromm (1957) describes self-care as "*the active concern for life and the growth of that which we love.*" If we want to accept ourselves, we need to start by being gentle and kind to ourselves. You must care for your well-being. You must confront yourself if you are unhappy. This is no simple task but "*one loves that for which one labors, and one labors for that which one loves*" (Fromm, pg. 21, 1957).

Self-Responsibility

This means that you are being *response-able*. In other words, you are positioned to respond to your needs without judgment, but from the perspective of care.

Self-Respect

This component means you are able to see yourself for who you really are and that you're aware of your own individuality and uniqueness. Having self-respect signifies that you have concern for your ability to grow and unfold as you are.

Self-Knowledge

If you do not know yourself, you can't respect yourself. "Care and responsibility would be blind if they were not guided by knowledge. Knowledge would be empty if it were not motivated by concern." (Fromm, pg. 21, 1957).

By now it should be clear that self-love is about action and not just a bunch of thoughts. Also, you need to make your well-being your core concern and act upon it.

A Prescription For Self-Love

Self-love is more than just a good feeling. It is an active state of gratitude and appreciation for yourself and your growth. It is a dynamic process through which we engage in actions that support our physical, psychological and emotional growth. Below is a little prescription to make sure you "dose" yourself with some self-loving action daily.

1. Schedule time for mindfulness practices.
2. Cultivate a mindset where you only act on your needs rather than instinctive wants to put others first.
3. Practice good self-care through cultivating healthy habits, such as diet, exercise, good sleep, making time for intimate connection, etc.

4. Remember to set boundaries (if you need to remind yourself of boundaries in more detail, flip back to Chapter 4).
5. Protect yourself by being mindful of the kinds of people you allow in your life.
6. Forgive yourself (more on this in the next chapter).
7. Ensure that you live with intention. Even if your purpose in life is not yet clear, you can set the intention to live a meaningful healthy life then align your decisions with that intention.

The more self-love actions you work on, the easier and more naturally that acceptance will flow, not only for yourself, but also for the current space you occupy in your life. Now that you love yourself more, you are probably in a space where you can forgive yourself.

But what about forgiveness for your toxic parents? Let's check out Chapter 7.

Chapter 7:

What About Forgiveness?

Now that you are en route to living your best life by leaving your past behind, do you actually have to forgive the transgressions in your past?

That is a question only you can answer. Forgiveness is ultimately your choice and yours alone. You do not have to let anyone pressure you into it. You can heal and move on in life without forgiving, but it all depends on you. Forgiveness in itself has a few good benefits. You have to weigh up if those benefits are worth it for you.

Forgiving our parents is a core task of adulthood because no parent is perfect. It is a slightly different story when it comes to forgiving a parent that almost destroyed you when they should have loved and cared for you. It is indeed important to forgive our parents, but it's equally as important to forgive ourselves for being a child and not knowing any better than our reality at that time.

What Forgiveness Is

Forgiveness is a choice to release resentment, hatred, bitterness or the feeling that we want to take revenge on the people who did us wrong. It is also a manner in which we find peace with the past. When we forgive, we make the decision to break the connection with our offender that is weighing us down. Forgiveness may be crucial if you reach a point where your peace is being destroyed by the ruminating thoughts of the people who hurt us.

Forgiveness is an act of strength when we know, can name and share our feelings in regards to what we need to forgive. This process can only happen when we have made clear we are hurt and when we carry no shame having been wounded.

Forgiveness is an act of stopping being victims of our past. It can help us take back control over our lives.

What Forgiveness Is NOT

Forgiveness is not pardoning, condoning, excusing an offense or forgetting about it. Forgiveness also does not mean that there needs to be reconciliation with your parents or parents. However, sometimes that naturally happens as part of the forgiveness process.

To forgive also does not mean that you have to forget. Though it may seem counterintuitive at first glance, the irony is that you can't forget if you want to move on. Pretending things never happened puts you at risk of it happening again. Sometimes you also need to remember where you came from in order to remind yourself of how far you have come.

Is Forgiveness Really Necessary?

Some would say *yes*, even if not for others, then for yourself. Some would say it's better to mourn the past than forgive the culprit. Reaching a place of forgiveness and cultivating it for yourself is a complex process. It is no easy journey.

Forgiveness is an active choice and it is something you have to be ready for. The deeper the wound, the more difficult the forgiveness process. Remember, forgiveness in itself is already hard, so to absolve your abusive parents for their actions will be especially hard. Those wounds were inflicted long ago and you've been walking with them all your life. Be patient with yourself. You may have to express some protest. You may have to be angry or resentful. Perhaps you will even have to punish yourself by holding a grudge for a while.

For a start, it's enough to consider the benefits forgiveness offers in overcoming negative emotions. Acknowledge the process isn't about the other person's benefit but your own. Once you have taken the time to validate your own emotions, you will know if you are ready to forgive. Remember, forgiveness is a choice for you, not something that your offender or parent is entitled to.

Chapter 8:

From Weakness to Strength - Finding Your Authentic Self

By now, you have a firmer grasp and grip on your trauma. You are at the point where you are almost eager to venture forth into the world with your new and "improved" self. Do you see the clean slate with endless possibilities in front of you? Can you feel the promise of love inside of you? You showed up for yourself. You are here to hold your hand from now on. You have armed yourself with all the knowledge you need to take a healthy step into the future. You have a new vision of the future.

This chapter will serve as a quick reference to which you can go back if you feel lost and need to find a sense of focus again.

You've reached a point where you really feel ready to let go of the past and move on. Oh, I'm so excited at the thought of the many new doors that will open up for you! Now is the time to believe in yourself and to grab new opportunities! You can make new explorations into yourself and the world around you.

Now you can live in the present without being overwhelmed by thoughts and feelings from the past. You have restored a feeling of safety and empowerment. You have let go (or perhaps you are still in the process) of emotions that held you back. Wherever your exact position may be, I don't know. But what I do know is you will notice an incredible inner shift towards being more accepting of yourself. I know that you have everything inside of you to walk in worthiness. You belong on this earth. You deserve to be loved.

It is time to embrace and honor where you've come from and what you've achieved so far. I hope you feel so proud of yourself. I urge you to take a moment to reflect on how big an achievement it is to be rid of trauma. Even if there still is some trauma lingering, applaud yourself for taking the first steps into managing the effects trauma had on your life.

As a last exercise together, I want you to sign another contract with yourself. The first one was a contract to commit yourself to your healing. You have done great. You may still have some healing to do but hey, only you will know when you can sign off that healing contract.

Next up we are signing a contract regarding the relationship with the new, healed you! Remember, this is just a draft. You can add and customize as you need. Onwards!

Contract:

A New Relationship With You (The Real You)

I, _____, acknowledge that from this day forward, I stand in a new relationship with myself. I have taken immense steps in my healing journey. I am proud to stand here: flawed, but worthy.

From now on, I will:

- Pay notice to my feelings, thoughts and bodily sensations. I will always work towards understanding my real wants and needs and I will respect them.
- Make new and healthy decisions for myself.
- Continue learning more about myself so I know better what kind of things I like and the kind of people I want around me.
- Keep on practicing self-love, self-compassion and self-care.
- Remember to regularly revisit my safe spaces.
- Build new and meaningful connections with others.
- Evaluate if my old relationships still suit the new me.
- Keep myself safe by recognizing toxic behavior when I see it and save myself.
- Be on the lookout for my own possible toxic behavior towards others. If I notice it, I will take the responsibility of addressing my behavior in love and kindness. I do not have to be an image of my parents.
- Rebuild trust in myself and others.

- Be gracious towards myself and give myself the benefit of the doubt.
- Acknowledge when I am doing the best I can and remind myself that that is enough.
- Remind myself that relationships do not have to be unsafe places.
- Join support groups where and when I need to.
- Give myself time and be patient. It's never easy to trust people again when one was hurt so badly.

I am proud of myself for undertaking this vigorous encounter with my own healing. Though I may not be fully healed, I am working at it. I know that I have everything in me to make it through. I am the primary adult and caregiver in my life.

I will keep these small promises to myself in this new relationship with the real me:

_____
_____
_____
_____
_____
_____

_____
Signature

_____
Date

Conclusion

"My mother said to me, if you are a soldier, you will become a general. If you are a monk, you will become the Pope. Instead, I was a painter and became Picasso."
- Pablo Picasso

Dear reader, I hope that you will be able to step into your name and become your own Picasso. You do not have to live up to your parents' expectations or the lives they want to live through you.

You have done yourself (and your children) the world of good by working through your childhood trauma as an adult. Now your children do not have to bear the burden of your unlived lives inside of you. You have taken up the challenge to come alive. To connect to the real you and live an authentic life.

If you found this book valuable, won't you take an authentic step towards the review button and drop us an authentic review! We'd love to hear your real voice!

Congratulations and thank you for taking this journey for yourself.

References

7 Steps To Accept Tough Situations In Life. (2013, December 3). Lifehack. https://www.lifehack.org/articles/communication/7-steps-accept-tough-situations-life.html

10 Rules to Help You Take Back Control of Your Life. (n.d.). Www.Healyourlife.Com. Retrieved August 13, 2020, from https://www.healyourlife.com/10-rules-to-help-you-take-back-control-of-your-life

11 Facts About Child Abuse. (2015). DoSomething.Org. https://www.dosomething.org/us/facts/11-facts-about-child-abuse

60 Minutes. (2020). Brené Brown: Focus on guilt instead of shame [YouTube Video]. In YouTube. https://www.youtube.com/watch?v=RSrXxqKfYwI

Anger and Trauma. (2013, October 23). At Health. https://athealth.com/topics/anger-and-trauma-2/

Bengtson, I., & read, P. L. updated: 17 S. 2019~ 8 min. (2019, September 18). 3 Stages of Healing from a Toxic Relationship with Your Mother. Psychcentral.Com. https://psychcentral.com/lib/3-stages-of-healing-from-a-toxic-relationship-with-your-mother/

Broadway, K. (2015, October 12). How to Create a Safe Place in Your Mind. Katherine Broadway. http://katherinebroadwaylpc.com/how-to-create-a-safe-place-in-your-mind

Chavez, H. (2016, January 2). 13 Signs Of A Toxic Parent That Many People Don't Realize. Lifehack; Lifehack. https://www.lifehack.org/350678/13-signs-toxic-parent-that-many-people-dont-realize

Chesak, J. (2018, December 10). The No BS Guide to Setting Healthy Boundaries in Real Life. Healthline. https://www.healthline.com/health/mental-health/set-boundaries#boundary-basics-and-benefits

Diamond, S., A. (2008, June 7). Essential Secrets of Psychotherapy : The Inner Child. Psychology Today. https://www.psychologytoday.com/za/blog/evil-deeds/200806/essential-secrets-psychotherapy-the-inner-child

Emotional Words. (n.d.). Retrieved August 18, 2020, from https://www.lovegrowbehappy.com/wp-content/uploads/2019/09/List-of-emotional-words.pdf

Flint, D. (2019, December 2). 3 Common Tactics of Manipulative Parents. Psychology Today. https://www.psychologytoday.com/us/blog/behavior-problems-behavior-solutions/201912/3-common-tactics-manipulative-parents

Formica, M. J. (2013, May 19). Self-Blame: The Ultimate Emotional Abuse. Psychology Today. https://www.psychologytoday.com/us/blog/enlightened-living/201304/self-blame-the-ultimate-emotional-abuse

Forward, S. & Buck, C. (1989). Toxic Parents: Overcoming Their Hurtful Legacy and Reclaiming Your Life. Bantam Books.

Fromm, E. (1957). The Art of Loving. George Allen & Unwun Ltd. http://www.filosofiaesoterica.com/wp-content/uploads/2017/01/Erich-Fromm_The-Art-Of-Loving.pdf

Gabbatiss, J. (2018, October 2). Child abuse leaves molecular 'scars" in DNA of victims' sperm, new study suggests.' The Independent. https://www.independent.co.uk/news/health/child-abuse-dna-trauma-genetics-molecular-scars-sperm-harvard-university-a8563906.html

Galor, D. S. (2011, December 8). Why do trauma survivors blame themselves? Dr. Sharon Galor. https://drsharongalor.wordpress.com/2011/12/08/why-do-trauma-survivors-blame-themselves/

Gibson, L.C. (2015). Adult Children of Emotionally Immature Parents: How to Heal from Distant, Rejecting or Self-Involved Parents. New Harbinger Publications, Inc.

Hall, K. (2012, July 8). Radical Acceptance. Psychology Today. https://www.psychologytoday.com/us/blog/pieces-mind/201207/radical-acceptance

Hammond, C. (2017, October 9). 7 Types of Parental Abuse | The Exhausted Woman. The Exhausted Woman. https://pro.psychcentral.com/exhausted-woman/2016/12/7-types-of-parental-abuse/

Harvard Health Publishing. (2019, February). Past trauma may haunt your future health -https://www.health.harvard.edu/diseases-and-conditions/past-trauma-may-haunt-your-future-health

Houston PBS. (2011). James Hollis PhD. Living Smart with Patricia Gras Understanding the Mid Life Crisis [YouTube Video]. In YouTube. https://www.youtube.com/watch?v=FHk8kWFIzYg

Johnson, E. B. (2019, April 15). Healing from Childhood Trauma: It's not impossible. It's just hard. Medium. https://medium.com/lady-vivra/healing-from-childhood-trauma-7f5b979a2631

Kos, B. (2017, July 17). Toxic Parents – Parents who do unloving things in the name of love. Agile Lean Life. https://agileleanlife.com/toxic-parents/

Lachmann, S. (2014, June 10). The 7 Stages of Grieving a Breakup. Psychology Today. https://www.psychologytoday.com/us/blog/me-we/201406/the-7-stages-grieving-breakup

Littleton, H., Horsley, S., John, S., & Nelson, D. V. (2007). Trauma coping strategies and psychological distress: A meta-analysis. Journal of Traumatic Stress, 20(6), 977–988. https://doi.org/10.1002/jts.20276

Martin, S., & read, L. L. updated: 21 O. 2019 ~ 4 min. (2019, October 21). 15 Signs You Have Toxic Parents. Psych Central.Com. https://blogs.psychcentral.com/imperfect/2018/07/15-signs-you-have-toxic-parents/

Medrut, F. (2018, January 23). 15 Most Enlightening Carl Jung Quotes. Goalcast. https://www.goalcast.com/2018/01/23/15-enlightening-carl-jung-quotes/

Mehlomakulu, C. (2017, September 3). Create a Safe Place. Creativity in Therapy. http://creativityintherapy.com/2017/09/create-safe-place/

Peterson, A. (2019, November 5). How to Change the Way You Talk to Yourself. Medium. https://medium.com/thrive-global/how-to-change-the-way-you-talk-to-yourself-c148c5441b69

Rebuilding Your Life After Abuse. (n.d.). See the Triumph. Retrieved August 13, 2020, from http://www.seethetriumph.org/blog/rebuilding-your-life-after-abuse

Robinson, L. (2019, March 21). Emotional and Psychological Trauma. HelpGuide.Org. https://www.helpguide.org/articles/ptsd-trauma/coping-with-emotional-and-psychological-trauma.htm

Selva, J. (2018, January 5). How to Set Healthy Boundaries: 10 Examples + PDF Worksheets. PositivePsychology.Com. https://positivepsychology.com/great-self-care-setting-healthy-boundaries/

Streep, P. (2018). Healing From a Toxic Childhood? The Two Words You Need Most. Psychology Today. https://www.psychologytoday.com/us/blog/tech-support/201801/healing-toxic-childhood-the-two-words-you-need-most

Taking Back Control of Your Life | Mental Health Recovery. (2018). Mentalhealthrecovery.Com. https://mentalhealthrecovery.com/info-center/taking-back-control-of-your-life/

Tartakovsky, M. (2018, October 8). 10 Way to Build and Preserve Better Boundaries. Psych Central. https://psychcentral.com/lib/10-way-to-build-and-preserve-better-boundaries/

The RSA. (2013). Brené Brown on Empathy. In YouTube. https://www.youtube.com/watch?v=1Evwgu369Jw

There Are No Toxic People, Only Toxic Behavior. (2018, June 15). Exploring Your Mind. https://exploringyourmind.com/there-are-no-toxic-people-only-toxic-behavior/

Tull, M. (2020, February 10). How People With PTSD Can Express Anger Constructively. Very Well Mind. https://www.verywellmind.com/constructive-vs-destructive-anger-in-ptsd-2797523

Understanding Adult Coping Strategies. (n.d.). Www.Blueknot.Org.Au. https://www.blueknot.org.au/Workers-Practitioners/For-Health-Professionals/Resources-for-Health-Professionals/Coping-into-Adulthood

Young, K. (2015, July 28). Stronger for the Breaks - How to Heal from a Toxic Parent -. https://www.heysigmund.com/toxic-parent/

www.ingramcontent.com/pod-product-compliance
Lightning Source LLC
Chambersburg PA
CBHW071446070526
44578CB00001B/235